WHERE'S THE JOY?

ENDORSEMENTS

"Danny not only writes about joy in such a way as to make fun fundamental ... but he puts wheels on it and feet to his faith, fleshing out the word he so winsomely writes. If you want to read about joy from a man who is mastering its practice, then let this book read you."

~Ben Courson,
Author of *Anthology of a Twenty-Year-Old-Soul* and
Founder of Hope Generation, bencourson.com

"Finally! *Where's the Joy?* is a sacredly simple book about reflecting, living and sharing joy. Williamson's down-to-earth writing style and biblical foundations are an encouraging reminder that joy is not in the choosing, but in the being filled to overflow by Joy Himself. Every page will bring a smile to your face and a deeper call to know Joy intimately and be changed for the better!"

~Bekah Jane Pogue,
Author, Retreat Speaker, Writing and Creative Coach, Spiritual Director-in-training and writer at bekahpogue.com

"God's will for you is to experience His joy—Jesus made that clear (John 15:11). But how? Are there Biblical instructions or principles that will help a person be more joyful? There are! And Danny Williamson knows them and follows them. And it shows! He is one of the most joyful people I've ever known. If you sense a lack of joy in your life, read this book!"

~Charlie Campbell,
Christian apologist and founder of AlwaysBeReady.com

"In a society that has so much bitterness towards one another because of conflicting views on life true Joy is absent. We try to find it in material or temporal things and are searching for a lasting Joy that cannot be taken from us because of time. Danny shares timeless joy in his book. *Where's the Joy?* couldn't have come at a better time than now. Believing in this truth that Jesus wants us to bask in his joy for us, knowing there have been people who have found it, and that it's attainable is a real reality! Danny gives us that in *Where's the Joy?* Thank you for this Danny, and I'm sure more will thank you for this timely read!"

~Jeremy Affeldt,
Three-time World Series Champion of San Francisco Giants and Co-Founder of Generation Alive generationalive.org

"Who knew that what the world was missing was joy? Danny's book is the glue society never knew they needed but something we have been searching for. We live in a chaotic and disjointed world that unconsciously is looking for answers to feel whole again. This book reminds us of the joy that God wants for each of His children. Simply stated there is no need to search for it. We need only to rediscover the gift that was given to us in the first place. Thank you, Danny. A higher power truly drives the words that flow from this book. Angels come in all forms ... even in a book about one simple subject ... JOY!"

~Deb Cantrell,
Executive Chef/Owner of Savor Culinary Services chefdeb.com

I absolutely enjoyed my friend, Danny Williamson's new book *Where's The Joy?*. What I loved the most was that this a book that Danny is uniquely gifted to write. Why? Because Danny is one of the most joyful people that I know. This book is a beautiful mix of delightful stories, profound insights and real life. Trust me, you'll find joy here.

~ Daniel Fusco
Pastor, Crossroads Community Church (Vancouver, WA)
and Author of *Upward, Inward, Outward* and *Honestly*
danielfusco.com

"If I was going to use one word to describe Danny Williamson, it would be the word Joy! Joy just exudes from the guy, which makes him a real gift to be around. One of the things I love about Danny is that he believes in a Big God who loves his people and is for his people and it is that belief that serves and the catalyst for Danny's joy, which is clearly expressed in the pages of this book. Danny speaks and writes from the heart and with a witty and down to earth style that is easy to relate to. This book will be a blessing and help to everyone who reads it!"

~ Rob Salvato
Lead Pastor at Calvary Vista

"*Where's The Joy?* Something I think all people desire is to be "happy," but how is that possible when life seems far less than ideal? Through Danny's stories and experiences of life's greatest great moments and the worst of the worst moments, he paints a beautiful picture of the true unending joy that is available in intimacy with Jesus Christ. This simple and yet complex truth is described in this book in tangible ways through stories, scripture, poetry, and much more, to make the reader truly reflect and understand the availability of a joy that never ends, fades, or wavers. This book is a great breath of fresh air that points to the everlasting joy found in a God who loves us."

~ Nate Dorman

Professional Surfer and Pastor of H2O Community Church

"Danny has managed to write a book that is simultaneously challenging and easy to comprehend. When I dove into reading it, I predicted this book would teach me about joy. What I didn't foresee was how it would wreck me and cause me to hunger for deeper levels of joy and intimacy with Jesus.

This wonderfully crafted book is going to be a tool that God uses to break the chains of depression in those who seek to rejoice in the Lord."

~ Alexandria Cooper

World Traveler, Author, & High School Student

"*Where's The Joy?* truly answers the question that deep down everyone's asking, and Danny does a remarkable job of communicating the extremely important concept that joy really is the solution for everything. This is both a lighthearted tale, and a profound message spoken with a refreshing vulnerability and authenticity. It is poetic and heartfelt, brought by a master in storytelling that will both inspire you and give you real tools to find and experience joy every day."

~ Mark Schneider

School of Ministry Director, Rock Church San Diego

"Read this book expectantly, for it will challenge your scope of how you can walk in genuine joy every minute of the day. Danny brings refreshing revelation that will lead you to be more connected to the Father's heart by refocusing on the biggest to the smallest details of what He has created for His children to enjoy."

~ Andrew Nielson
Managing Director, YWAM Colorado Springs

Where's The Joy? is an incredible reminder that joy awaits us in ALL seasons. Danny Williamson teaches us the art of noticing where joy can be found and how we are to access it despite our circumstances. If you want to improve your ability to find joy in your life, this is the book for you!

~ Lance Villio
President, I Am Second
iamsecond.com

"Finding a book that celebrates the path that I am in with my life can be challenging. I have recently realized that my darkest of pitfalls was what allowed me to make the greatest of triumphs. It's a life journey that's hard to mirror on those who need the guidance who are just starting on their path.

Danny, you really have a way with becoming vulnerable to the reader, reflecting on your life in a way that's easy to envision, but substantial enough, make a full circle to connect the dots back to joy. As a touch onto chapter 5; I too am happy you are here with us today. You have a lot of joy to bring on to this world. High five buddy!"

~Aspen Luzier
Founder, Rebel for a Change
rebelforachange.com

DANNY WILLIAMSON

WHERE'S THE
JOY?

An invitation to look up, reach out, and
experience life's greatest treasure

NEW YORK

LONDON • NASHVILLE • MELBOURNE • VANCOUVER

WHERE'S THE JOY

An Invitation to Look Up, Reach Out, and Experience Life's Greatest Treasure

Published in New York, New York, by Morgan James Publishing. Morgan James is a trademark of Morgan James, LLC. www.MorganJamesPublishing.com

ISBN 9781642792102 paperback
ISBN 9781642792119 eBook
Library of Congress Control Number: 2018908511

Scripture quotations are taken from the Holy Bible, New Living Translation, copyright © 1996, 2004, 2007, 2013 by Tyndale House Foundation. Used by permission of Tyndale House Publishers, Inc., Carol Stream, Illinois 60188. All rights reserved.

Cover Design by:
Jordan Freund

Interior Design by:
Christopher Kirk
www.GFSstudio.com

Morgan James is a proud partner of Habitat for Humanity Peninsula and Greater Williamsburg. Partners in building since 2006.

Get involved today! Visit
MorganJamesPublishing.com/giving-back

To you, Michelle Ann. The joy of my heart.
My wildflower, butterfly, sunrise.
To my 3 wonderful boys, Isaac, Malakai, Josiah ...
May you know fullness of joy and abundant life!

CONTENTS

FOREWORD

By Jeremy Camp

I've had the privilege of being friends with Danny for almost twenty years. We met as young bros in California after I finished bible college and we had the most amazing group of friends who were genuinely in love with Jesus. We jumped at any opportunity we could to worship, serve and minister together. We are all still in ministry and continue to stay in close contact with each other, which I'm convinced is because our foundation was one of wholeheartedly pursuing the Lord in close community.

Danny is such an amazing story teller and truly brings joy wherever he goes. He always has a story like none other you have heard, and often has the whole room in hysterical laughter, at whatever the cost.

When I found out he was writing a book about joy, I thought he would be the perfect person, because it is an attribute that describes him so well. I'm honored to call him my friend and I am fully confident you will be deeply ministered to by his heart and such a needed message for our world today. We are in desperation for more joy, but not in the way our culture or society dictates it to us – as a continuous thirst for something that will never be filled, but in the treasure and hope that is unwavering despite what is going on around us, because it is rooted in eternity. May your heart be overwhelmed in the best way as you dive into the chapters of this book.

PREFACE

I'm excited to go on this journey of discovering joy with you. Thank you for responding to the invitation to look up, reach out, and experience life's greatest treasure! Here's to seeing abundant, lasting joy in your life.

Each chapter contains two main elements:

PROSE

Stories, thoughts, and insights to support the chapter's theme.

POETRY

I recently heard how the mind and soul benefit from reading poetry. So, at the end of each chapter, I'll share poetry to help you go deeper in your journey to experience a life of joy.

CHAPTER 1

HALF N' HALF

Introduction

I really like half n' half in my coffee. It knocks the edge off the bitterness, turns dark liquid into a creamy brew, and the tan color reminds me of my wife's gorgeous skin. I guess you can say I like my coffee like I like my woman, "hot and brown." Joy is a lot like half n' half. It reduces the bitterness, turns darkness into beauty, and reminds us of the wonderful gift of life.

This first chapter is also like half n' half. You'll get a taste of what you're getting into with some traditional "book intro" stuff. But you'll also get some first chapter flavor, so that you can jump right into the joy. Plus, if you are like me, you might tend to skip book introductions, and it would be a bummer if that happened. So, let's leave room for cream and add some joy to this cup we call life.

THE SEARCH FOR WHAT EVERYONE IS ASKING FOR BUT CAN'T IDENTIFY

We all want some …

People like joy, but sometimes they don't know how to put a name on it. We want to experience a joyful life, but it may seem like a fallacy or unattainable Christmas bonus. Our world is searching every possible avenue for joy. Billions are looking for a happy and satisfied life. Their search comes in all shapes and sizes. Climbing the corporate ladder, swiping through Tinder, binge shopping on Amazon Prime, vegging out on Netflix and Hulu, or pursuing another online degree. We play endless rounds of golf, take another Carnival Cruise, sip extra doses of gin and juice, attend the latest self-help retreat, and read *The Book of Joy* by the Dalai Lama and Desmond Tutu. Thinking, "If I just do 'this' today I will be happy." But we still come up short. We run on an endless treadmill, pursuing satisfaction and fulfillment. We are insatiably hunting for lasting happiness and don't even realize it.

Let's step back for a second, and ask: "*What* am I trying to find?" Most likely, it's joy. Joy is not a new concept, just a forgotten one. We are hungry for it. The longing for joy is increasing. Many are starting to ask the hard questions, write the books, sing the songs, and pen the poems in the pursuit of joy. Even still, joy remains a bit of an untouchable mystery.

Leading me to ask, *Where's the Joy?*

MY QUEST FOR JOY

Backed by life experience, research, and sincere desire, this book is broken into three sections to help us discover and live in lasting joy: Responding to Wonder (theological aspects of joy), Joyful Narratives (our testimony of joy), and At Our Fingertips (the availability of joy).

Approaching life with awe and *wonder* is rare these days. Maybe we just need to look up. Our eyes are often transfixed down into the virtual world of social media. And we are missing it. When was the last time we paused long enough to see the sunset or watch a leaf fall from a tree? I've begun to think if we take the time to look up—we might even see God. And when we discover the beautiful personality of God, joy becomes our story. As one smart theologian stated, "God alone is the only adequate center for human existence, and He alone can enable us to experience life with joyous spontaneity and to relate to others with love." I agree.

Joy can also become a *narrative* of our life. We can have stories of victory, poems of deliverance from darkness, or songs of hope before an on-looking world. Even amid life's most significant storms, joy can be present and active in our life. It's actually possible!

Real joy is much more *available* than we may realize. Joy doesn't have to be a distant memory or a forgotten dream. It's ready for the taking. We may need to hop off the couch or stretch out our hands to get it, but we need to realize joy is literally at our fingertips.

Joy ... we all want some. We need some. It's time for a breakthrough. Not the hyped-up fabricated stuff seen through rose-colored glasses and an overpaid televangelist. I'm talking about the radical and immovable joy, which doesn't fade when life hits the fan. Joy is more than an emotion or feeling. It is a lifestyle we are invited to live daily. But maybe we think our invitation got lost in the mail. It's time to open the mailbox, tear open the envelope, and see the message from Jesus Himself, which says: "I have told you these things so that you will be filled with my joy. Yes, your joy will overflow!" (John 15:11).

A FEW PERSONAL REASONS WHY I WROTE THIS BOOK

Joy is something I personally long for in my life. My guess is you crave joy too. Nobody wants to live life in the dumps.

I don't claim to have it all figured out. But I have discovered ways to bring joy into my home, workplace, and relationships. In a way, this subject of joy has become my life's work. Not just jokes, humor, and blessing but deep, supernatural joy. How and why do we experience it? What opens the doors to joy and releases it to fly? Why is joy such a mystery? How does it give me strength? If it's available for me, why do I still wake up frustrated, perplexed, or broken?

Nevertheless, I often find myself resisting the God who created joy. This God *of* joy. Sometimes we run back into the darkness and neglect the beauty of His love, grace, hope, and forgiveness. Why? Am I really that selfish? What is my problem? Why do I refuse to look up from my phone and settle into virtual hypocrisy or darkened fantasy? Sometimes, it's easier to hide in shame; resisting the vulnerability and gratitude, which lead to lasting joy. Oddly enough, joy is so easy to recognize in my friends, family, co-workers, and even strangers. This journey to remain in joy is a mystery.

Even more, joy seems to be a topic seldom explored in-depth. Finding a book devoted to the topic of joy is hard. We may discover traces of joy in blogs, books, or articles, but the subject remains somewhat ambiguous. It has been over 2,000 years since the birth, death, and resurrection of Jesus. Why is joy often missing from the discussion? I think it's time we start talking about it more. Because I've come to realize, joy is life's greatest treasure. Joy is our strength. Joy is more than daisies on a warm summer afternoon.

Our country needs some joy. Our world needs some joy. Particularly, today's younger generation seems to be craving joy. Longing to laugh. Desperately seeking something or someone to make them happy. What will satisfy? What will cause us to wake up happy? What will break the chains of depression, anxiety, fear, or loneliness? Through life experience and research, I've concluded: only the *joy of God* can set us free. We try to find it outside of God, but I just don't think it is possible. When we have faith, guess what? We have joy. When we experience love, we have joy. When we walk in hope, joy fills our hearts. Joy is the result of faith, love, and hope. Joy is even one of the "fruits of the Spirit." When we are filled with the Spirit, joy is the outcome.

Taking this leap of faith doesn't mean we are immune from heartache, shame, or failure. It doesn't mean we have it all figured out. But the joy of God does mean we can access an indescribable kind of hope, which frees us from pains, perversions, and broken promises.

The bottom line is: *joy* – really – helps – people. We need it. And we can have it. And we don't have to fake it. We can *live* in the supernatural wonder of joy daily. In the good times and the bad. It's true.

Ultimately, my hope in writing this book is to bring God's joy to the world. I believe there is something the world needs to hear. It is JOY. It will be our strength in this dark and lustful hour. Joy is our hope in today's perilous and deviant times. I want people young and old to experience supernatural joy. I must know why man, at the end of his days, longs not for joyous pleasure, but *joyous meaning.* Imagine the peace he'd feel the day he died if he could say, "I brought my family hope and lasting *joy* because of this life I lived."

In this process of writing about joy, I experienced a renewed desire to discover how joy uncovers the meaning of life. I penned some thoughts down one night and wanted to share it. Here is a piece of my heart:

Sheesh. I am 40 years old. How am I already in the middle of my life? What will the second half look like? Will I make a dent? Will I bring a smile to a face? How will I live out these next 40 years? How will I make a difference? Will joy shine through how I speak, write, work, or live?

If I do not wake up in the morning, would those who knew me, loved me, and walked this life with me say: "*JOY*?" Will my wife know I loved her? Not the fluffy or infatuated kind of stuff, which only lasts a couple of years. The real agape kind of love. Will she know I *chose* to love her, embrace her, forgive her, and encourage her? She is a daughter of God. Purchased by His blood and redeemed by His hand. She is the woman I chose to spend my days with every day. She is the one I chose to vow with, laugh with, cry with, and possibly even die with. If I happen to take my last breath before she does, how will she remember me? Would she wake up missing the sound of my breath in the night or my early departure every morning? Would she recognize my absence at the dinner table on weekday evenings? Would she know and understand my choice to stick it out through thick and thin to raise this family with her? Our marriage covenant was and still is ... a choice.

Love is a choice. Purpose is a choice. But *joy* is the result of our choices to love and live a purposeful life. When I choose to love, joy is the outcome. When I choose to live with purpose, joy is the legacy. When I choose to respond to the reality of Jesus, joy writes my story.

Am I living with this type of response to His reality and presence? Have I decided to *not* fake it till I make it, but rather – surrender to God's greatness in life's biggest storms? Does eternity feel the difference of my response? Do my children experience joy, laughter, and hope through my life? Do my friends witness joy in me? Do my co-workers and ministry partners encounter joy when I am around?

Will joy mark my life?

I want it to.

Maybe you have similar questions. I'm tackling this mystery and going on a bit of a treasure hunt for one of life's greatest gifts. I would love for you to join me.

JOYFUL ANTICIPATION

Will a joyful expectation be spoken, more than tokens for the broken?
Life of casualty, longing for reality –
story, bringing joyful glory
to the One who makes me ...
What will be said of this personalized narrative?
Real and true, seeing past and viewing through
stained glass windows on the other side of pain.
The epitaph meant to last – into legacy choices
of agape, grace, and freedom songs ...
Joy is lived, longed for, embraced.
Taking me to the place of deepened reality,
surprising generosity, and fascinating complexity
of meaning, purpose, wonder, and choice.
The choice of horizon views, beyond the shame,
choosing the Name ~ above all names, to proclaim
to the masses ...
Yet, as time passes,
Too quick to notice a smile before me,
the mid-life crises unfolding,
or the wife of youth I'm called to be exploring.
Making the choice of joyful transformation,
daring to dream and imagine ...
the beauty of relationship,
with a Joyful Galaxy Builder
who braved the elements of heartache and pain
to risk His story, legacy and name,
to love a sinner like me ...
I have a joyful anticipation ...

PART 1
RESPONDING TO WONDER

"When the poet Carpani enquired of his friend Haydn, how it happened that his church music was so cheerful, the great composer made a most beautiful reply. 'I cannot,' he said, 'make it otherwise, I write according to the thoughts I feel: when I think upon God, my heart is so full of joy that the notes dance and leap, as it were, from my pen: and, since God has given me a cheerful heart, it will be pardoned me that I serve Him with a cheerful spirit.'"

– John Whitecross Anecdotes

CHAPTER 2

THE EPIDEMIC OF TEXT NECK

Look up, look out, look around ...

The sweet romance of baseball. There's nothing like it. No clock, the freedom to spit, perfectly mowed green grass, red dirt, leather gloves, wooden bats, and 40,000 fans eating overpriced hotdogs and drinking $12 beers. Fathers and sons sing side-by-side during the seventh inning stretch, rally flags wave in the wind, and the smell of peanuts fill the air. America's pastime. I know baseball has lost some flair since the 1950s, but the sport holds a special place in my heart. Some of my fondest memories were at the Ball Park. We lived about three hours from Candlestick Park in San Francisco, so my dad was infamous for pulling me out of school early to see our beloved Giants. High fives all around, cheers and tears, thrill and heartbreak. With great anticipation, every year we hoped our team would win it all. The last time the Giants won the title was in 1954 when my Pops was two-years-old. So, it was a long time coming.

November 1, 2010 was a night I will never forget. My wife endured the drama as I turned on the TV to watch my San Francisco Giants battle the Texas Rangers in the World Series.

Since I literally waited my entire life for this moment, it was a big deal.

After battling through the past five games of the series, the sights of victory began to become a reality. Our closer Brian Wilson was on the mound with his fearless trend-setting, shoe-polished beard wafting in the breeze. It was his moment to shine. History was about to be made. The pitch to all-star catcher Buster Posey was on target to strike out the Rangers' Nelson Cruz as the Giants clinched their first championship in 56 years. The ballplayers and coaches began to race around the mound and hug each other like school children in a bounce house. Our living room turned into pandemonium with chips flying and couch cushions launching across the floor. I scooped up both of my boys, screamed from the top of my lungs and jumped around the house. In my state of testosterone-driven excitement, I failed to hear my three-year-old son Isaac reeling in pain. I had inadvertently almost yanked his shoulder out-of-socket during my celebratory lap around the house (I still apologize annually for my outburst and his shoulder incident).

Still, I couldn't believe it.

Victory …

Just minutes later, my Dad called with his whopper voice shooting through the phone, "Danny, I've waited my whole life for this! Hum baby, they finally did it!" We looked up to the screen and it was official. The victory was secure. The city of San Francisco went ballistic as the party began. Millions showed up for the Victory Parade, and it's as if the entire city took a massive exhale. Finally! It took 56 long years, but the wait was over.

This moment in time is one I will always remember. My Dad's excited phone call, the victory parade, the city-wide celebration, and the long-awaited road to victory reminded me of some spiritual truths: God. Heaven. Joy. Hope.

The Bible describes God as a Heavenly Father. When His Only Begotten Son, Jesus, overcame the domination of sin and death, I believe He shouted through the courts of heaven, "I've waited all eternity for this!" Finally, we can celebrate! Jesus was the Grand Marshal of the parade. The angels rode through streets of gold singing songs of freedom. Through Jesus' masterful work on the cross and rolling away the stone an early Sunday morning, death lost its grip. Sin lost its domination of humanity. *Joy* marked heaven's hallways as the trophy was raised up high.

SOMETHING TO CONSIDER

As we embark on this rescue mission for joy, I want to tackle *theology* right off the bat. What is "theology?" Isn't that a word saved for guys attending seminary? Not necessarily. Theology is less complicated than we think. Theology is *thinking about God*. Studying God. Talking about God. A. W. Tozer describes a theological concept as he considered the fact that "God waits to be wanted ..." Just the simple act of wanting God is a form of theology.

I even think agnostics and atheists are theologians. They may be trying to deny God's existence or neglect His presence, but in doing so, they are also on a theological journey. The Christian seeking answers for suffering in the world, and his agnostic college roommate who blames a Higher Power for such suffering, have something in common. They both are investigating God. Both are seeking to know who God is, even if they have yet to believe in Him. Given this truth, theology isn't something we need to be afraid of or ignore. Theology is one of the most fundamental facets of our existence.

This is the reason I believe good and sound theology produces abundant joy. As we *look* unto Jesus, the Author and Finisher of our faith, we find *His* joy awaiting us. The personal joy of Jesus is available to all who are willing to look upon Him. Are we ready to explore this God of joy with some investigation and genuine inquiry? The cool thing is, there is no grading system with true biblical theology. I like how my friend Jarrid phrased it, "Religion wants to see your report card, but Jesus wants to see your heart." A good theological study isn't meant to stroke our intellectual egos, so we can flaunt a Ph.D. or be called a Master of Divinity. Instead, theology should result in a renewed mind, a captivated heart, and a joy-filled lifestyle.

DISCONNECTING CONNECTORS

With that said, are we willing to put down our phones and look around? Our Instagram account will still be there. Our Snapchat opportunities can wait. Responding to the text may need to hold off until tomorrow. Maybe, looking up from our cellular world would save us a few chiropractor visits. Perhaps, we'd notice some extra giggles from our kids. And maybe, even build some better friendships. Years ago, my grandpa Norm said something about cell phone use, when he wrote a Haiku called 'Disconnecting Connectors.' Spot on. The first step to having stronger friendships and connecting to God may require a small step of faith by disconnecting from our phones. Simply looking up and around. We may even find "joy" posted on the scoreboard.

In fact, new research reveals how our screen-time is dramatically undermining our parenting efforts, romantic relationships, and even our interaction with God. One recent study is showing how a toddler's ability to learn new words declines when mom or dad is interrupted by a cell phone call.

The study also noted how young athletes' performance drops when their parents are on their phones instead of watching their children on the playing field. "Children ran faster and were more physically coordinated when their parents were available and responsive compared to when they were absorbed in using their mobile phones."

It's not just parents developing text neck. Generation Z youngsters (those born between 1995-2012) were born into a virtual world, resulting in what psychologist Jean Twenge refers to as "an epidemic of anguish." Twenge describes how social media has caused those in Gen Z to experience poor emotional health and lack of preparation for adulthood due to their average daily use of five to six hours with online media (texting, chatting, gaming, web surfing, streaming and sharing videos, etc.).

Regardless of age, I believe as a society, we are neglecting the wonder of our surroundings. We are losing our sense of awe and of life happening in front of us. And it's beginning to rob us of our joy.

REGAINING A SENSE OF WONDER

As I sit down with my warm cup of coffee and a hint of half and half, I look out the window to see wind casting its blanket upon the water, ducks drifting along its slow currents, green grass nestled by its shore and silver-lined clouds painting pictures against the canvas of blue sky. I think I see Him. God's grin is peeking through His creation, waiting for us to notice Him. He sits quietly. He waits. He anticipates. Who will take a breath? Who will notice me? Who wants me? You see, *this* is theology. Taking moments out of our busy lives to pause, listen and look. God may not be asking you to read Wayne Grudem's *Systematic Theology* or memorize Walter A. Elwell's *Evangelical*

Dictionary of Theology, but He *is* asking you to look up. Look around and see the beauty.

Yes, the digital world we live in is fascinating. You can take a picture, have a video conference, buy an airline ticket, quote Martin Luther King Jr., text your girlfriend, and boomerang the most recent coffee shop experience within a 45-second time span. Technology is phenomenal, and I sing right along with Kip from *Napoleon Dynamite*, "…I still love technology, always and forever."

Nevertheless, there is so much more to see in life. Think of how a child is amazed by the simplest things. Having this childlike wonder happens to be an early stage of theology. Observing life with awe shows us how little we are and how enormously big God is. If we would just look up, we may taste a bit of wonder. In the moments when we question our purpose in life, remember childlike awe and wonder. As Ravi Zacharias states, "A sense of wonder is indispensable to having meaning in life." When was the last time we tried to count the stars, smell our toothbrush, or interact with an orangutan at the zoo? Whether it is awesome or awful, life gets exciting when we discover the awe.

If we step back and think about it, God is at the center of wonder and awe. I like what Francis Chan said in his well-read book *Crazy Love*, "It's crazy, if you think about it. The God of the universe – the creator of nitrogen and pine needles, galaxies and E-minor – loves us with a radical, unconditional, self-sacrificing love. And what is our typical response? We go to church, sing songs, and try not to cuss." I see his point. It is time to go a bit deeper than the church hymnal or trying not to say s*#@ when we hit our thumb with a hammer. Let's look at this dynamic universe and the allure of God's unfathomable love with child-like wonder and awe. Wonder is where theology begins to make sense. Awe is where the inquiring mind, the investigating heart, and the inquisitive soul starts to find answers. Look up. It builds a case for theology, leads us to a deeper knowledge of God, and results in a life-demonstration of joy.

SELAH MOMENTS

If we pause long enough, we can discover endless details about God. I remember sitting in class with a thought-provoking Bible teacher named George. He challenged the class to pen 100 attributes of God on a sheet of paper. Bible verses from children's church came to mind. The sweet sound of my sister singing a Whitney Houston song floated in my thoughts as I started my list. Love, hope, mercy, grace, truth, purity, compassion, beauty, patience. The page began to fill up as I wrote down His character traits. And then one descriptive which kind of surprised me: *Joyful.*

Wait a second. Double take. Jesus is joyful? Yep, sure enough, it's true. Jesus said, *"MY* joy." God likes to laugh, smile, chuckle, and celebrate life! God Himself enjoys sunsets, a toddler's giggle, all-star drum beats, and the delicious scent of freshly baked bread. The more I think about this, the more excited I get. Does this mean the Creator of the Universe likes campfires, guitars, and ice cream? Yep! Is Almighty God fond of basketball, pour-over coffee, and father/son wrestle matches? You got it … He loves them! This is because every good and perfect gift comes from Him. He designed all these things for us to enjoy because He delights in them. As the Psalmist declares, *"You feed them from the abundance of your own house, letting them drink from your river of delights."* He leads us to His river of joy. All the really good stuff in life was His idea. When we recognize He is the mastermind, we can look up, give Him the glory, and go bananas with life. His joy contributes to some marvelous medicine, my friends!

I really desire to begin intentionally looking for joy in the face of God. I want us to embrace the idea of God Himself being *joy*. It seems like a good place to start as we step into this quest for joy.

I WONDER

I Wonder ...
What would happen if I look up?
Will faces be seen, open eyes dream, or life redeem –
the over-distracted monopolies of time?
Will disconnected connectors finally connect with heart's desire
for connected community?
Will birds sing again, will playgrounds swing again, before
notifications chime on my phone again?
I Wonder ...
What would happen if I look up?
Will daylight dawn, will paintings be drawn, or will I be withdrawn
into my virtual-world of social so-called popularity?
Will I see flowers in bloom, children dancing in the living room, or
helium-filled balloons ~ dancing through the sky to catch my eye
as time floats by?
Will the sun set again, before death begins, trapping breath within –
while my online world closes in?
I Wonder ...
the outcome if I look up?
Will beauty be noticed, will mountains be moved, will life begin?
Will joy unravel upon the road less traveled, if I look up to the face
of my Friend?

CHAPTER 3

YOU DIDN'T HAVE TO DO THAT!

Autumn's beauty is a feast

Recently my family and millions of onlookers throughout the United States experienced a solar system phenomenon with apocalyptic brilliance. The total solar eclipse on August 21, 2017, in Nashville, TN was something to behold! With flickering light beams peaking around the moon, a 360-degree sense of sunset and complete darkness in the middle of the day, all one could do was sit in awe. The Great Artist was behind this wondrous display, no doubt. He captivated the attention of entire cities, business executives and homeless men. Onlookers paused their rat race of life and encountered a raw and unmatched demonstration of beauty.

During those two minutes of artistry, I thought, "God, you didn't have to do that!" But I sensed Him gently whisper, "Oh yes I did!" He didn't have to display His handiwork to a nation, which so often forgets Him, but He did. This is who He is. He wants us to encounter Him in the everyday and the spectacular. He wants us to enjoy the wonder of His creation. He wants us no matter how often we dismiss Him. As I pondered how

God communicates with us through shooting stars and solar eclipses, I remembered Psalm 19:1-4:

The heavens proclaim the glory of God.
The skies display his craftsmanship.
Day after day they continue to speak;
night after night they make him known.
They speak without a sound or word;
their voice is never heard.
Yet their message has gone throughout the earth,
and their words to all the world.

The silence of the total solar eclipse in Tennessee spoke volumes. It caused our preoccupied world to be still and hear the declaration of God's glory. I imagine moments like these are the expressions of a *joyful* God!

FLOWERS

My wife loves chips and salsa. She even prefers a bag of tortilla chips and fresh Pico de Gallo over a bouquet of wildflowers. I love the look on her face when I have those restaurant style chips behind my back and hand her the goods. Brownie points for me every time!

Every so often though, I know it's time to venture into the flower shop because flowers capture romance, tenderness, and beauty. I love bringing my wife a bouquet of calla lilies, orchids, or tulips. Tulips; though, are my favorite. Don't criticize bro. (A side note to the fellas reading this. Know your flowers man. It can light candles in the heart of your wife or girlfriend one day.)

Surprising Michelle with some fresh-picked purple tulips taught me a valuable lesson one spring day. We placed the slightly droopy tulips gently into their vase on the dinner table. Before sunset, these puppies perked up and were in open bloom.

If your unfamiliar with the details of a tulip, let me tell you, you're missing out. As I admired the tulips, I noticed the beauty of the outer violet shades. When I glanced inside the bulb, the real magic happened. Goodness, gracious! I discovered a perfect mathematical equation of yellow strands decorating the inner aspects of the flower. It was wild. I couldn't help but say, "You didn't have to do that!" Lord, this is the inside of the flower, the part passed by 98 percent of flower children and overlooked by 95 percent of thankful wives. You did not have to design such perfection in hidden places. These are the fun, joy-filled glimpses of God in the details. *His* joy can be found in the overlooked pockets of creation.

FISH

Flubby is his name. He recently enjoyed his first birthday in an oversized Mason Jar and is part of the Williamson family. Flubby is a dark blue betta, also known as a Siamese fighting fish, and he is my friend. After all, he is the first pet we've had in our 14 years of marriage and was purchased for our son Josiah's second birthday. I get to feed his little wiggling self as his floaty fins waft through the water to munch on shrimp pellets. He is a creation of God and worthy of notation. A marvelous fish I must say.

Spending six months at sea with the U.S. Navy familiarized me with flying fish. Every time I stepped onto the flight deck or the bow of the massive ocean war-time vessel, I would look down to the splashing waves and see these crazy little fish flying out of the water. It was beautiful and entertaining all at the same time. I looked at the endless horizon of open sea and couldn't help but think about my Maker. He didn't have to make those little flying fish. It wasn't necessary. The sunrise or sunsets would have been enough. But His character goes the extra mile.

Have you ever swam with a ghost pipefish or a blue-ringed octopus? Me neither! The intricate details of these hardly-seen fish are remarkable. Take the ghost pipefish for instance. Part of the Solenostomidae family, these fish range from ornate to robust to hairy. As masters of disguise in the coral reef, with multifaceted and rainbow colors, these fish must be one of Jesus' favorites. How could He not have chuckled and smiled when He created this group of sea creatures?

His joy radiates throughout every corner of creation. If we take a moment to pause and look below the surface, we can experience the very joy of God.

FOOD

Speaking of fish, I have an avid love for fresh sushi rolls, sashimi cuts of yellow-tail and grilled salmon—most of the time that is. After returning from a five-month trip in India, a parasite or dysentery had annihilated my stomach. I spent over 150 days in the country and lost more than 20 pounds. Maybe it was from the blue-chicken curry or the goat intestine, which occasionally showed up on my plate. India is amazing, and the hospitality is even overwhelming at times. But for us Westerners, the cuisine can be taxing on our stomachs and gastrointestinal tracts. Upon returning to the U.S., I was eager to gain back some weight and grow back my American fat face. I was on a mission to grind on all-you-can-eat sushi, a double-double at In-N-Out and even some of my mom's world-famous lasagna. But to keep with the fish theme, I'll share the wonder of my "meet-the-parents" story.

Given how happy I was to dive face first into the nearest sushi bar, I was thrilled to meet Michelle's family at a local Japanese restaurant in La Verne, CA. I was a bit nervous but relaxed when her dad hit his face on the restaurant door when we walked in. There was some bleeding, but he handled it well. We sat down for our meal once we knew he wouldn't need stitches. Since my wife is of Filipino background (and fish is a major staple in the Filipino diet), the table was set for me to make a killer first impression. So, I hit it hard and ate everything presented. I was in full chow-down stride when my attempts to dazzle came to an end.

After consuming all the salmon, spicy tuna, and yellow-tail, we moved on to Japanese dessert. I felt accomplished. Smiles broke out across the table from witnessing Danny's ability to consume large amounts of exotic, raw fish. Then … it happened. After swallowing my last bite of green tea ice-cream, I felt a tummy rumble followed by an immediate hot flash. I knew I was in trouble. I took a quick trip to the restroom for some relief. Nobody noticed my restroom run, and soon after, everyone was getting ready to leave. I was giving my first hug goodbye when a 185-degree hot flash burst across my body. I knew there was calamity ahead. I told Michelle's parents and sisters I needed to take a quick bio break. Well, about 25 minutes later, I was still there. My experience on the porcelain throne was long enough for her sisters to bail and her dad to knock on the door to see if I was still alive. Then this adverse reaction turned a page as my tongue and lips began swelling up and red splotches spread across my belly. Oh, snap! I was now amid an unconventional allergic sushi shock. My fearful future in-laws rushed me to the nearest CVS Pharmacy to guzzle some Benadryl. Let's just say; it was a long night. Especially since I spent an additional 30 minutes in the CVS bathroom wondering if I was about to meet Jesus face to face. It wasn't one of my finest first impressions!

Despite my near-death experience, I still acknowledge how food is a pure gift from God. Fortunately, my allergic reaction to sushi was just a one-time thing. Hallelujah! I love that stuff. I believe Jesus anointed Japanese cuisine with flavors from heaven. Food brings joy to so many situations. God designed it this way. It's part of His beautiful, creative genius. Whether it's chicken enchiladas, carne asada burritos, or slices of watermelon, food is a verifiable tool of thanksgiving and joy. Food can draw us closer to the thoughtfulness of God. The late southern humorist Lewis Grizzard described the joy food brings by stating, "It's difficult to think anything but pleasant thoughts while eating a homegrown tomato."

Besides tasting good and filling our bellies, food also has a fantastic way of bringing people together. The greatest benefit of traveling the globe is enjoying the company of newfound friends while feasting on cultural masterpieces. Whether it is a boiled hairy pig with potatoes in Uganda, a Shabbat Dinner of fresh bread and hummus in Israel, or empanadas and a glass of vino in Argentina; we should enjoy meals with other people.

So often, due to the fast-paced nature of our lives, we fail to slow down long enough to sit around the table with some burgers and beverages, leave the cell phones in our pockets, and turn the television off. It's time to connect. Life is too short. The dining table is where we make memories, kids come alive, and wives feel most loved by their husbands. The patio tables, picnic blankets, and park benches are connection zones of joy.

Seasons of life in Latin America taught me the irreplaceable value of the dining table. For us in the United States, it is common to quickly pop up from dinner to tackle dishes, move onto the plan for the evening, and if lucky, scarf down some brownies and coffee. Then company leaves, and we enter our private lives once again. Conversely, in most Latin American countries, dinner means fellowship, long conversation, stories, and laughter, not just a checkbox marked on our list. What is the rush? Why are we so quick to move onto the next thing? Food should beckon us to connect and celebrate joys in life. It's one of the primary reasons God created food. Cesar Chavez nailed it by saying, "If you really want to make a friend, go to someone's house and eat with him … the people who give you their food give you their heart." What do you say we slow down a bit, share some food, and share our hearts? Lost joy is bound to be discovered when we come to the table.

MUSIC

Now here is an idea of God, which completely blows my mind. Music. It touches the heartstrings, moves the emotions and stirs the soul to tears, laughter, or giddy transparency. Music is a worldwide phenomenon, reaching every culture on earth. I've even tested the waters in my travels across nearly every continent. I love to ask everyone the simple question: "Do you like music?" 100 percent of the time, the answer is … yes! It can be people from the urban jungles of Kunming, China or the residents of small Moroccan villages in the High Atlas Mountains; everybody digs music.

I think it's because music reaches raw emotion and the deeper meaning of life, where words come up short. Music takes us on a heart journey, triggers daydreams, and even moves us into action. Music creates moments and memories every day. It can be the high school prom, a cross-country road trip, or a night by the fire. Music is a marvelous and collective experience for every listener.

Let's start with love songs, which represents the most common lyrical content for music. Heart-break, new love, proposals, intimate communication, and the list goes on. Romance drives musical inspiration, and I thank God for this. I can't tell you how many times Jack Johnson has got me out of the dog-house after a tiff with Michelle. I just turn on 'Better Together,' 'Banana Pancakes,' or 'Angel,' and we soon forget our troubles. Then there is the deep, wedding song material like Josh Groban's 'When You Say You Love Me' or Sade's 'By Your Side.' The music moves two hearts into one and creates dreams of affinity. Music can strengthen friendships and even bridge broken walls of trust. When we use music the right way, it is a powerful tool.

But music can also lead us down a road of tremendous sorrow. Like whenever I hear 'November Rain' by Gun's & Roses, I go down a dark path of early pubescent drama. I recently downloaded the hit song to see if I would remember the feelings of being dumped by that blonde girl in the eighth grade. Yep. Still there. Or when I hear 'Black' by Pearl Jam, I am immediately transported to the emotional baggage of teenage pain. Then there is the overwhelming sadness when I hear 'Tears in Heaven' by Eric Clapton. Dang. Clapton wrote this tune in tribute to his four-year-old son who died in a devastating accident. I read he still can't perform the song in front of a live audience. It is just too painful. Music takes us to unimaginable emotional places.

Certain melodies can also bring back fond memories. Heading to a P.O.D. or Dogwood concert was a common thread of my early 20s in San Diego. We jumped head first into the mosh pit and crowd surfed to let off emotions, uncontrollable hormones, and young rage. I always felt better after vent sessions at those concerts. It's because of the music. I could forget my circumstances or heartbreak and get lost in the music. It was an outlet for grief and avenue to escape.

Then there is Jazz. Big-Band Jazz makes me reminisce about watching my Dad fire off a drum solo. I was often the roadie at his local concerts or weekend gigs. Such cool memories. Jazz jams are a great way to mellow the mood or wind down the day. It even makes an elevator pleasant. I just love it.

How about 70s Funk? Oh, snap! I've learned over time if Funk-tunes get rolling, the dance floor attendance doubles. Mark my words. Next time you are at a wedding, ask the DJ to throw down some old-school Funk and see what happens. It gets the party going every single time. My buddy Mark would agree. He loves Funk so much he had his wife walk down the aisle to 'Sissy Strut' by The Meters. And the best part of this story is the wedding was in Bangalore, India. I'll never forget looking over and seeing my bro with a cool smirk on his face as he watched his bride come down the aisle. All his future Indian family members appeared incredibly perplexed by the music selection. It was fantastic! Music helps etch these memories in our minds.

If you ever wonder the draw of music and its influence upon the world, take some time to watch the recent Wembley Stadium concert by Ed Sheeran. Regardless of some of his lyrical content, it blows my mind how one guy and one guitar can fill a stadium with 80,000+ fans for three nights straight. It's because of the music. Incredible.

Even though music holds the power to do good, there are also a plethora of shady tunes out there, influencing people to despair or angst. The devil is real, and he will use anything to rob us of God's goodness and love. But God is the One who created music. God designed music to give us a pathway to joy and to experience Him with deep intimacy. Both in lament and triumph, music is an "instrument" – playing songs of joy throughout our stories.

Most importantly, let's talk about musical holy moments. Like the Sunday morning worship service followed by communion, prayer and embraced humility. Or the late-night car ride with my buddy Douglas in Mar del Plata, Argentina when Hillsong United comes on. Tears and emotion. Or the home bible study where everyone is sitting on couches or kneeling on a carpet as they sing out a love song to Jesus. The Call gatherings in San Francisco, New York City, or Washington D.C. where 20,000+ young people fast, pray, and worship for 12 hours to seek revival in our nation. These holy moments, all led by instrument and song.

Music is a gift.

This donation of God leads me to crawl under a chair and clutch my bible as the worship leader strums his guitar in melodic rhythm. Or dance around my living room in my t-shirt and boxers before my Heavenly King. These are some of the holy reasons Jesus created music. To let go of the to-do list and the work just to be with Him. I believe joy is His primary objective in giving us music.

I have the privilege of working with a professional musician who loves Jesus. I get to travel with him a few times a year, sleep on a tour bus and wake up in a new city every day. We drink good coffee, snack on bowls of cereal and shower in a bathroom the size of my closet. But after a day or two, we all start missing our wives and kids. Even still, each night when it's time to plug in, I see the power of the Gospel through music. I see tears, feel the presence of God, witness my buddy and the band pour out their hearts to Jesus and even hear a few thousand people sing in one voice. But the best part of it all—is seeing him live out the lyrics of his songs. You can see the hurts and the healings in his everyday dealings. Music is just the outlet he uses to share his story with the world.

Imagine what life would be like without music. What would a movie be like without a soundtrack or musical effects? We can thank God for how music elevates every experience. He invented B-flats and F-sharps. He gave us the insight to create the mandolin, piano, drum, guitar, bass, cello, ukulele, oboe, saxophone, trumpet, tuba, high-hat, Cajon, microphone, and Hammond B-3 organ. He did it all for our enjoyment and pleasure. All for us to have an outlet for our ever-changing moods and emotions.

He didn't have to create music.

But He did.

For you. For me.

Within our recent research of joy, my book editor Nicole noticed how music takes us on a God-designed journey to experience supernatural joy. Psalm 5:11 says, "singing births joy." In fact, throughout scripture we see songs deliver joy, and we see joy become singing. When people worship together, something magical happens. Everyone brings their different backgrounds and enters one conversation together with God. Music is a brilliant tool God created to help us see who He is. Lyrics and instruments can point us to Jesus, who can handle our disappointments and turn our pain into joyful noise.

To get a musician's perspective, I got ahold of a longtime friend who gets to sing, write lyrics and play music for a living. You may know him. His name is Phil Wickham. I've known him since he was about 13 years of age and have seen Jesus touch his life with a gift bestowed upon a select few. He can sing like the wind. His gift of songwriting and music has touched millions. Michelle and I even had the privilege of him singing at our wedding in 2004. Phil is the real deal, I've seen him live out what he sings, and it is a genuine treasure to know him. I absolutely love this guy!

My first question for Phil was, "Why do you think God created music?"

Immediately, I heard an extra spark in his voice, as he described how music is a *gift* to humanity. "Music is a beautiful, yet unnecessary gift God has given every civilization throughout history. He didn't have to give us this gift, but He did. Music has a way of giving a voice to an entire community, creating a sense of unity in the heart. And for Christians, this unified voice gives us a great picture of what heaven will be like."

I wanted to get a bit more personal, so I asked, "What are some ways you experience God when you sing, play an instrument, or listen to music?"

He painted a great visual and explained, "Music seems to be a magical bridge between our emotions and the real physical world. Thus, when I sing or play an instrument, my voice has a way of reminding my heart and emotions of who God is. Singing about how great He is, or how He is a good, good Father strengthen my heart and life."

To tie joy into music, I asked him, "What is the most joyful part of playing music and leading worship?"

He candidly replied, "I am continually writing songs, and exploring ideas with music. But nothing is more joyful than when I 'land a song' and introduce it to my local church. The real 'Aha! Moment' happens when the audience connects with the melody, the lyrics, and the presence of God."

Those moments of connection with Jesus can be "easier" when we are at church. I wondered how he maintains a lifestyle of worship beyond the tours and stage?

"We simply welcome worship music into our world as a family. We play it at our house. The kids hear it as they're playing Legos. Now, I'm not saying worship music is the only thing to listen to, as there are tons of amazing and beautiful pieces of music throughout the world. But there *is* something to be said about *worship* music. It reminds my family and me of God. Whether I'm taking a jog, washing dishes, or cooking dinner with my wife, music continually reminds us who God is."

My final question to Phil was tied into the previous one, "For those of us who aren't musicians or songwriters, how can we practically use music to create an atmosphere that enables us to press into who God is and experience His joy?

His answer was simple. "Push play. Whether it is on our smartphones, during our morning routines, or while the kids are playing with their friends. Welcome the musical worship of God in our personal space. Doing so is a great conduit for experiencing the joy of God through music."

Thanks, Phil!

These are just a few of the reasons why music plays such an important role in our discovery of joy. Lasting joy has music intertwined through every nook and cranny, every turn and signal, every heartache and celebration.

God didn't have to give us music.

But He did.

And one day, *He* is going to sing a song over us. I like what the Old Testament promises in the passage, "For the Lord your God is living among you. He is a mighty savior. He will take delight in you with gladness. With his love, He will calm all your fears. He will rejoice over you with joyful songs."

The transformational leader Nehemiah proclaimed similar encouragement to the people by declaring, "Go and celebrate with a feast of rich foods and sweet drinks, and share gifts of food with people who have nothing prepared. This is a sacred day before our Lord. Don't be dejected and sad, for the joy of the Lord is your strength!" Joy leads us to victory and strength. Let's take a moment to stop and smell the flowers, notice the fish, savor food, and listen to the music. Like Judy Harrell said, "The sweet smell of lilac trees, the warmth of summer's breeze—tell me you are not far away." Noticing the simplicities of His creation brings us into the wonder of His presence. And as we will say a few times throughout this book, the fullness of joy is found in the company of God.

CREATION SPEAKS

Creation speaks ~ where words fail to reach
into the heart of imagination,
leaving us breathless, speechless, questioning
what completes us ...
Solitary tree placing a canopy of beauty ~
over rock and ocean ~ recognized as alone and lonely,
yet casting a story for all who pass by.
Do we stop and stare? Or quietly prepare to move on?
Creation speaks ~ what sight cannot breach
the boundaries of emotion with a touch of a hand,
strolls through sand, or voice of fellow man ...
Even boundaries of darkness abandon their power ~
with the caress of rain, a stroke of lion's mane, or taste of grain
upon one's lips as she sips
on the cup of His redemption.
Creation speaks ~ the joy of His ideas ...

CHAPTER 4

THAT'S NOT MY NAME

Redemption & Fatherhood ...

After a friend's wedding in Central California, we drove down I-5 in my wife's 4-Runner with our baby Isaac snuggled in his car seat. Two hours into our drive I was ready for fresh coffee. With Isaac in tow, we stepped into a Starbucks off the freeway. To my surprise, one of the greatest basketball players of all time, Boston Celtic hero Bill Russell, was waiting for his vanilla latte. How could this be? Bill Russell is a basketball icon with 11 NBA titles, five Most Valuable Player awards, and a lifetime supply of NBA socks and t-shirts. But for some reason unknown to man, instead of exchanging pleasantries, I went blank. Despite my love for basketball and knowledge of NBA history–I was dumbfounded. Still, I walked up to this incredibly tall individual and said, "Excuse me, sir, what is your name again?" He quickly fired off, "Don't worry about it ..." Oh, snap! I desperately racked my brain while we waited for our coffees. Finally, I heard the barista call out, "Bill." Refusing to waste my only chance to talk to this NBA legend, I turned back to this towering 6'10" giant of a man and said, "Excuse me, Mr. Walton ..." Immediately, his eyes burned with a bit of fire, and he snarled, "That's not my name!" At this point, I had to walk away in shame, realizing it was the one and only – Bill Russell, NOT Bill Walton.

I called the legend of professional basketball by the wrong name! And I was really, really, really, wrong! For those who know basketball, I have no excuse. I failed ... but for those who don't know, it is like calling Magic Johnson by the name of Larry Bird. Bill Russell, an NBA great and a voice in the civil rights movement of the 60s, continually defending the rights of African Americans. Whereas Bill Walton is the ultimate tie-dye wearing, extremely white-skinned, hippie-type, Hall of Fame basketball player. Did I blow it or what? Well, at least they were both tall professional basketball players. A true epic fail.

I think sometimes we do the same thing with God. We call Him someone He is not. We allow fears, insecurities, and doubts to fog our vision of Him. When life takes a turn, do we look up and say, "What's Your name again?"

"I can't handle this! I can't handle this job, this marriage, this stubborn child, this debt ... Why is this happening to me?" Somewhere along the way, we heard "God won't give us more than we can handle," but that's a kind of a crock. I feel like God gives me things I can't handle every single day. Disappointment can cause us to look at Him with grimace, anger, and worry. We may even start to call Him the wrong name.

When we look at God from partial truth or biased preconceptions, we jump into rationale just like I did with Mr. Russell. I got the first part right: Bill. But I gravely missed the second half and identified him with someone he is not. We understand the first part of God's name: God. But how are we filling in the second part?

God _____?

How do we fill the blank? Maybe it's God "doesn't like me," or God "is mad at me," or God "is unfair." But with gentle kindness and maybe even a tear in His eye, He responds with, "That's not My name." And unlike "Mr. 11 Rings," God doesn't walk away in a huff with a bruised ego. Rather, He stops in tracks of grace to state, "My name is blasphemed all day long. But I will reveal my name to my people, and they will come to know its power. Then, at last, they will recognize that I am the one who speaks to them."

He reveals His name and character to all who will listen. While running on the treadmill this morning I heard His voice whisper in a song. Instead of blasting my usual Twenty-One Pilots or Coldplay jams, I turned on some Jesus Culture. The song echoed His truth singing, "Joy has a name. Joy has a name ... Jesus."

He knows we misjudge Him, shame Him with our words, and mistake Him for someone He is not. And still, He pursues us. He persistently knocks on our door, asking us to hear His voice of truth declare, "I am JOY ..."

GOD ENJOYS REDEEMING PEOPLE

Sometimes people have a rough start in life. Really sucky stuff. Some children wake up daily to angry and abusive parents. Kids are jumping from one foster home to another. And some don't know where they will get their next meal. Hurt, pain, and loneliness set the course for sin to invade innocence. Eventually, this sin leads to dark paths of bitterness and tragedy.

I don't have answers for the inordinate amount of suffering in the world, but I have noticed how sin is always involved. We live in a fallen world dramatically influenced by sin. It started with Adam and Eve in the Garden, and it continues with us today.

Sometimes, I am overwhelmed by the pain in this world. It even makes me want to cuss a little. Well, a lot. Nevertheless, there is always hope. "To all who mourn ... He will give a crown of beauty for ashes, a joyous blessing instead of mourning, festive praise instead of despair."

When I forget such promises of redemption, I remember my friend Ole. Rather than plagiarize my buddy, I wanted Ole to share his story in his words:

I considered my life normal. Looking back, people actually looked at me with pity. At a young age, my life spiraled into chaos and poverty. My mom's infidelities and drug habits sent my Dad packing. We were always moving, and she was endlessly changing boyfriends. My three siblings and I were just along for the ride. Garbage and dirty clothes littered the floors from my mother's all-night parties. We went into scavenger mode as we got ready for school each morning. One morning, my only clean option was a karate gi I got from a donation center. In retrospect, dirty clothes would have been better. That day, I got the full brunt of childhood meanness. Kids laughed as I stood in line for the free breakfast, which I looked forward to each morning. Some kids even threatened to fight the "karate master." Thankfully, an older kid protected me that day. I never got his name, but I was grateful. What I thought was just another day of third grade, became one of my worst memories. It shifted my outlook on life. The laughter I endured echoed shame and isolation. I realized I was the dirty, unwashed, poor kid who always had lice. I went home crying. One of the kids said, "that's why he can't go to birthday parties." It was true, and I knew it now.

One of the boyfriends we moved in with lived in a partially gutted and torn down home. It did have a roof and rooms. Mostly; though, I remember the metal claw-foot tub. This guy made us kids hold books over our heads and beat us if we dropped them. He loved the belt and used it often. Finally, the police got involved when he messed with my younger sister. Off we went to another new place, then another.

Each time the guys got seedier, and conditions worsened. Another boyfriend made us kids sleep in his van outside. He said he didn't want kids, so we were only allowed inside to go to the bathroom. At one point, we lived in an abandoned trailer, which had a massive hole in the bathroom floor. Animals got into the house at night if the bathroom door was open.

My siblings and I kept getting sick. I watched my mother give my brother a cup of dish soap claiming it was Kool-Aid. She told firefighters he just did that kind of stuff and she was concerned for his wellbeing. It was weird seeing her transform into a caring mother for an audience.

In that same place, one of her boyfriends' brought home kittens, and we got to keep two. One died in the machinery underneath the rocking chair while her boyfriend was in it. All of us kids cried. A few days later, my mom brought me outside to show me something she found. It was my dead kitten, with its head caved in. I did not respond; she knew I knew she did it.

Another incident with a boyfriend led my frantic mother to walk us kids down the side of the highway to move yet again. The police picked us up. After that, we stayed with our aunt and uncle for a short time. My sister stayed longer because of an agreement with my mother. Whenever the state inquired, my aunt and uncle lied. We later learned my aunt and uncle were brutally molesting my sister.

By this time, my father wanted to reconnect with us kids. When he saw our living conditions, he tried to get custody of us. My mother said no because we were her source of income. My dad finally convinced her to let us visit his home. We were shocked by his normal home that night. We considered staying, but while we were away, she called saying she kicked her habit and prepared Christmas. No one answered the door when we returned home. Once inside, we saw engine parts on the living room floor. Her violent, convicted child molester boyfriend was asleep on the couch in his underwear. Our mom finally came out of her room angry, calling us traitors. She threw a bag at us and returned to her room. Inside were three pencil holders with single tone keyboards. We sat in our dark room playing those tiny keyboards all night ... I can hear the tone even now.

Finally, we testified against her and moved in with our dad and stepmom. They loved us and put us in church. I was glad for my new life, but I just played the game. I was hurt. I didn't want to be touched and was mad my mom didn't love me.

I started carrying a knife. I envisioned killing my mother to see sweet justice served. I got into partying and ecstasy; I liked how it seemed to make everyone loving. Still, I knew something was missing.

Eventually, Jesus got my attention. I gave my life to the Lord at a Billy Graham crusade. Billy referenced Psalm 27:10, "when my father and mother forsake me, then the Lord will take care of me." I felt alone and betrayed by the world and my family. But God cared. I felt His love as well as the joy only Christ can bring.

I was shocked when God called my wife and me to take a mission trip to India. Before leaving, we spent time in the mountains to hear from the Lord. We each separated for an evening and I had a scary moment when I saw a bear. I had the knife, but who was I kidding? The knife just made me a poky snack. Frozen in fear, I heard God speak loud and clear. My life was a series of sprinting from one thing to the next. I had friendships but no deep connections. The only person I truly cared about was my wife. I was harboring bitterness in my heart.

For years, I ignored "why" I held onto my knife. But God wanted to chip away at the deepest parts of my heart. Salvation was easy, I accepted and followed. This spiritual growth part was hard! Could I really forgive my mom? I let my tears fall, and when the sun came up, I used a rock to hammer my knife into a tree. The knife represented my harbored un-forgiveness. I left both behind in the woods.

After the night in the wilderness, God moved big. I no longer waded into the waters of the Spirit, I allowed the current to carry me. I finally had the joy, which I had admired in so many friends (like Danny) and it was awesome.

I saw God work miracles in India. When I returned, I began serving full-time in youth ministry. Missing out on my childhood made investing in youth a joy. My family and I are now in Oregon planting a church to share the love of Jesus and the joy only He brings. Best of all, I have a family full of love and laughter. My journey has been (is) crazy, but God turned even those locust-eaten years into a tool to bring hope. Joy is not in our circumstances but in our savior Jesus. He brings joy, peace, and purpose. Looking back on my pivotal moment in the wilderness, I understand how forgiveness is essential for true joy. Those believers you see with a gleam in their eye have walked the pathways of forgiveness. From one sinner to another, let go of bitterness and step onto a better path.

THIS is a story of redemption. Only God can transform such pain into purpose. Jesus, the Redeemer, brings joy in the morning and hope for a new day.

God is bigger than the pain. He can redeem the darkest soul, the troubled past, the misunderstood mind, the broken heart. Just ask the Psalmist who declared, "You have allowed me to suffer much hardship, but you will restore me to life again and lift me up from the depths of the earth." Sometimes we walk through valleys of pain and suffering. But take heart friend. He is the redemptive remedy. Elizabeth Elliot, widowed in the jungles of Ecuador through the martyrdom of her husband Jim, stated this challenge, "Where does your security lie? Is God your refuge, your hiding place, your stronghold, your shepherd, your counselor, your friend, your Redeemer, your savior, your guide? If He is, you don't need to search any further for security." Take a deep breath. He enjoys restoring the lost. The redemptive story of Job speaks to the value of trusting him through thick and thin. Job lost it all; yet, trusted his Redeemer. The results were evident "… the Lord restored his fortunes. In fact, the Lord gave him twice as much as before!"

God is in the restoration business. He did it with Job, Elizabeth Elliot, and Ole. He redeems people. He redeems purpose. He replaces tears with a smile, a broken heart with a beautiful song, years of sorrow with an eternity of joy. He enjoys redeeming people, even nations. Israel, with its history of brokenness from rebellion and sin still has a promise of redemption. "O Israel, hope in the LORD; for with the LORD there is unfailing love. His redemption overflows. He will redeem Israel from every kind of sin." The same is true for you and me. He can redeem us from every kind of sin. Wrongs can be made right. He can turn our stress into strength, our burden into a blessing, and our hurt into happiness.

GOD IS A GOOD DAD

Fortunately, I have a great dad. He has been there for me through thick and thin, loved me unconditionally, listened to my struggles, given advice, and picked me up when I've been down. He would win the Dad of the Year trophy again and again. He is one of my best friends, loves Jesus with all his heart, loves my mom, and pays for dinner when we go out to eat.

As a 6-foot-2-inch eighth-grader, I had vain hoop dreams of being the next "Pistol" Pete Maravich or Steve Nash. While shooting hoops in my backyard one sunny afternoon, I cut to the baseline and drove through an imaginary defender for a monster jam layup. Seconds later, I was rolling on the concrete. I heard a dreadful snap, crackle, and pop from my ankle. I shouted for my 85-year-old neighbor Harriet to help. But to my surprise, my Pops came rushing to the scene. He then scooped up my large teenage mass in his arms to carry me to his truck. Before I knew it, I was whisked away to the E.R. for x-rays. Something dawned on me that day. I had an amazing dad. Mustache and all, he was my new superhero. He was willing to carry me, listen to my never-ending girl problems, and journey life with me. I am forever grateful for his Jesus-style love, patience, wisdom, and genuine friendship.

But there is a sad side to this story. More than half of our society does not have a healthy relationship with an earthly father. When some of us hear the word "Daddy," our hearts cringe with fear, rage with anger, or recall painful memories. When someone recalls memories with their dad, resentment builds. Or we feel pangs of jealousy watching a father push his daughter on a swing at the park. Why wasn't he there? Why did he leave? Whether it's an absent or an abusive father, many young hearts feel abandoned by their dad. Sadly, our earthly father impacts how we view God.

When we hear "God Almighty," we are fine. When we hear "King of Kings," we roll with it. When we hear "Prince of Peace," we take a deep breath. But when we hear "Father" or "Abba" (Hebrew for Daddy), many can't relate. Our minds wander and brew feelings of frustration and bitterness. We question God's goodness. We wrestle with love, affection, and security. We struggle with identity, confidence, and truth. We have major daddy issues, and we blame it on God. Dad wasn't in the picture growing up, so why would a Heavenly Father be?

But the truth is, God, desires to father us. As Donald Miller describes in his wonderful memoir, *Father Fiction*. Growing up with the absence of an earthly dad, Miller recognized this struggle. However, through time and friendships, he saw how God as the Father gets joy by "giving us joy." God enjoys bringing a smile to our face. He enjoys holding us when tears fall from our cheeks. He enjoys watching us shoot hoops in the backyard. He enjoys watching us color in our coloring books. He likes you. You are not a burden to Him.

He cares about the little things too. Maybe the pain is still pretty deep from "dad" not being around. The missed ball games, the empty rocking chair, the vacant seat at the dinner table, the nonexistent pillow fights.

The importance of having a dad really hit home when my friend Jeshu shared a crazy experience in leading a discipleship school in Chico, CA. Jeshu is an open-to-the-Holy Spirit kind of guy, making way for some sweet breakthrough for students. During a time of prayer and worship in the class, he heard a gentle whisper from the Lord, "Ask Jenny if she would like a piggy-back ride!" A bit weird, I know. But Jeshu couldn't shake God's subtle request. So, with necessary tact, he followed through. "Excuse me, Jenny, I feel like God wants me to give you a piggy-back ride around the room?" asked Jeshu. "Ummm. I guess so?" she replied. Fortunately, Jeshu is one of the most trustworthy guys on the planet, so she went for it. Laying aside all awkwardness, she jumped on his back. They leaped around the room as students giggled watching this unusual moment unfold. After a lap or two around the room, the giggles quieted. Chuckles became sobs. Jeshu's shoulder turned into a landing strip for tears.

This act of faith helped a precious, young college girl find healing. She grew up with an absent father, and never experienced the joy of being silly with her dad. She always wanted to clutch her daddy's neck on a piggy-back ride as he ran around the room and bounded up the stairs. Our Abba Father knew her pain well and decided it was time to step in. He is a Father to the fatherless. He is a healer of broken dreams. God revealed to His daughter how He really is a good, good, good, Father. He does care. He cares about the small details and tucked away desires. He cares about what makes us smile or brings us laughter. He sees you, and He cares.

This Heavenly Father I speak of, whispers our name with comfort and love. The birth of my second son Malakai reminds me how a father's whisper makes all the difference. Thanks to the wonders of medical technology, my wife had a smooth birth process after receiving an epidural. However, when this little guy arrived, his screams reached opera levels, and his chubby purple face squirmed with angst. He wanted back inside the comforts of the womb and everyone needed to know. Why am I suddenly buck naked and cold? Seriously though, imagine being taken out of your cozy warm bed and thrown into the snow with your neighbors seeing your butt. It's pretty humbling. The nurses cleaned him up but knew it was time for Daddy to step in. I came over to his frightened little body, placed a blanket around him, and whispered, "Malakai, Daddy's here. I love you, buddy. It's going to be ok." No joke, as soon as he heard my voice, his crying hushed, his fears subsided, and he calmed down.

I believe the Lord is whispering the same to some of you today. "Darlene, I've always been there." "Jason, I will never leave you nor forsake you." "Amy, you are the apple of my eye." Sometimes we don't see Him, feel Him, or recognize He is there, but He is. We all desire the warmth of human touch in the form of a dad. But God's warmth is always near. We have hope. As the Psalmist declares, "Father to the fatherless, defender of widows — this is God, whose dwelling is holy. God places the lonely in families; He sets the prisoners free and gives them joy." To the 85 percent of prisoners raised in fatherless homes, God can be the dad we always longed to have. To the 90 percent of runaway children who lacked the presence of a father, God calls out with an aching voice, "I can give you joy." The kind of joy only a dad can give.

FATHER

Father, friend ~ redeeming the end.
Words describe emotions inside when love has found His home –
to reside, dwell, imagine, unfold.
Hope and song sing along-side angels declaring a whisper –
of purpose and peace to the pain.
Father, friend ~ redeeming the end.
Lovely His-story unfolding on pages, written through ages –
of time alongside patience describing His children at play.
For His way makes ways without a way –
to share suffering cups with a grin.
Father, friend ~ redeeming the end.
How can waking dreams once so dark become these beacons of hope?
How can tear stained pillows speak to mornings of joy?
How can water turn to wine, life come from death, or fears
become love over time?
My Father, my Friend ~ redeeming my end.

PART 2
JOYFUL NARRATIVES

"The world is not going to pay much attention to all the organized efforts of the Christian church. The one thing she will pay attention to is a body of people filled with a spirit of rejoicing... When the Holy Spirit is operating, this is the inevitable result – a joy which is unspeakable and full of glory."

— Martin Lloyd Jones

Writer's Block

Scene 1

Sometimes when authors are working on a story, they get what is known as "writer's block." Just stuck and unsure how to move forward. The narrative pauses and creativity halts. The writer might need to step back for a second and evaluate some things. I think we can get writer's block in life as well. When life gets crazy, and storms wreak havoc, we get stuck. Something keeps us from living the joyful life God has called us to live. What is hindering my story from unfolding?

Let's evaluate our Joyful Narrative and discover what's blocking, hindering, or contributing to our promised path of lasting joy.

CHAPTER 5

ROOTS IS A LONG MINI-SERIES

Sucking life or giving it ...

High school was an interesting time for me. I didn't follow Jesus until my senior year, so the first three years were confusing. Puberty struck early in junior high, so I walked into my freshman year at 6 feet 2 inches tall, with plenty of armpit hair and a freshly trimmed mustache. I was dating the prettiest girl in school as a frosh. I was a starter on the football and basketball teams, voted "most popular" in my eighth-grade yearbook and was ready to rock the boat of Upper Lake High School. My sister was a hip upper-classman, so I even was invited to keg parties and was part of the *in*-crowd. My confidence level was at a nauseating state. I was the man.

But it wasn't long before my status changed. I dropped a touchdown pass during a homecoming game and played for a basketball team that lost nearly every game. Adding to this string of disappointments and losses, my pretty girlfriend dumped me. She was enjoying the attention of the senior fellas a bit more than mine. They didn't drop touchdown passes. They had chest hair and thicker stashes. I was devastated. Some seeds of depression took root during the earlier pubescent years of middle school.

And by the time these freshman failures hit, I thought suicide was the answer. I'm not sure why I went to this extreme, but I did. I figured suicide was my way out of this emotional roller coaster and the answer to my broken heart.

Insecurity raged in my emotions at this time. But somehow, I masked my pain with humor and an outgoing personality. On the outside, I was a happy, fun-loving kid. But depression was sinking in, and dark clouds hovered over my heart and mind. What many did not know, and many still don't know, is I tried to take my life on multiple occasions during this season. Whether it was tying a belt around my neck, taking unprecedented amounts of ibuprofen, or running up a nearby mountain to ponder cliff jumps, I thought killing myself would solve my problems. I was only 14-years-old.

The truth is, suicidal inclinations have no age range. I recently had a conversation with a social worker specializing in childhood suicide. She said the youngest case she treated for suicidal attempts was just eight-years-old. No matter your age, your emotions matter to God. Your sadness may seem small or trivial to others, but feelings of anguish are real. It makes me want to listen to my kids a bit better. They have fears, concerns or stresses, which matter to God. They should matter to me too.

Fortunately, my parents were attentive enough to notice my struggles. I knew my emotions mattered to my mom and dad as they patiently loved me through this time. I vividly remember my mom sitting on the edge of my bed, *listening*. Her willingness to hear my fears, struggles, and my mental battle brought me through. So, by the grace of God and these loving parents of mine, my suicidal efforts didn't work. I'm still alive. I'm pretty sure my wife and kids are glad my attempts were unsuccessful. Parents and friends, may I offer a bit of encouragement? *Listen. Just listen.* So often, this simple act can save a life. It saved mine.

As time went on, suicidal tendencies were no longer the norm, but the pain of my broken heart was still there. I tried anything and anyone to numb it. When my high school hormones raged, I thought sex would hide my insecurities. I soon realized getting naked with a girl only unmasks anxiety and self-doubt. I also thought intoxication would take the pain away. Every party and drug grabbed my attention. I clung to my hurts and tried to desensitize them on a dark and empty road. This road led me to daily bong rips, beer pong sips, mushroom trips, and shallow relationships.

By my junior year of high school, I went from being the second fastest guy on my football team to the second slowest! Talk about a turn for the worst. Drugs rapidly took their toll on my body and personality. I can still hear Coach Kinser yelling during sprints, "Unhitch the trailer, Williamson!" Things only grew worse. My GPA dropped from 3.5 to 2.2, I was dating a hippie chick addicted to meth, and my extroverted personality sank into a melancholy quote of, "You want to smoke a bowl?"

My 'wake-up call' arrived when I was caught in the school bathroom puffing the magic dragon. I was suspended from school for a week and threatened with expulsion.

My Dad wasn't too happy about this path I was on. So, during my week of suspension, he arranged for some sober self-reflection. He told me I would create a driveway in our front yard with my hands. No shovel. No rototiller. Just my hands. Maybe he figured since I liked weed so much, I should pull some out of our yard with my fingers for a few days.

My goodness. This arduous work taught me about one thing – *ROOTS.* The thing is, if we don't get rid of the roots, the plant stays alive. The weeds grow back. The tree stump remains. Both good and bad roots can impact our joy. The bad roots suck the life right out of us. The good roots sustain life, build strength, and produce fruit.

BITTER ROOTS

The 1977 epic mini-series "Roots," became one of the longest and most popular television mini-series in history, with an estimated 100 million people watching the finale on ABC. Viewers were forced to reflect on the painful path of slavery, which still stains our nation's history with bloodshed, sadness, and remorse. Since the series covered 150 years of a painful storyline, the show needed a running time of 570 minutes to uproot the history of our nation.

These deplorable roots of injustice are painful to recall. They mark the social health of our nation even today. These are the bad, life-sucking roots, which are grounded in the soil of hatred and bigotry. These roots rob our country of peace and tranquility. These bitter roots grow hatred, racial outbursts, and city-filled riots. These unearthed roots of pain are robbing our country of joy and enslaving us in the process. These roots divide us and; ultimately, destroy us. As James Baldwin stated, "I imagine one of the reasons people cling to their hates so stubbornly is because they sense, once hate is gone, they will be forced to deal with pain."

Bad roots extend beyond the national or historical scale. The same type of bad roots can affect us on a personal level. We hold onto roots of fear and rage, feeding the soil with insecurities and shame. We resist forgiveness. We grow anxious. We harbor anger towards those who hurt us. The roots grow deeper into our hearts, minds, and actions. The fruit of our relationships rot, the flowers of communication wilt and our commitments break. The truth is, we can only hide these roots for so long. It's just a matter of time before others begin to taste the rotting fruit and smell the decaying flowers. Friends begin to shy away from us. Our children start to grow less comfortable around us. The joy of marriage begins to diminish. When we allow these toxic roots to grip our hearts, we let resentment define us and shape our lives. Our bad roots start producing weeds, which eventually take over God's garden of joy. But God didn't intend for us to live in a weed-covered garden full of rotten roots. He wants more for us.

RADISHES

I really like vegetables. Lettuce, carrots, and asparagus to name a few. There is one veggie; however, which I just can't wrap my mind around. The radish. The word "radish" even sounds mean. It's a bit spicy and bitter. Why would I want a bitter root in my fresh salad from Whole Foods? It hits the palate with a weird twist and disturbs the taste buds. And even if we enjoy radishes in our salad, do we grab a plateful of radishes as a snack? We don't, because it is a *bitter root*.

Much like the funky tasting radish, *bitterness* is an emotional root. Bad things have happened to us. Spouses have cheated. Babysitters have molested. Parents have bailed. There are a million reasons to be angry. Why did this happen to *me?* Resentment festers, pain increases, and roots deepen. We harbor the pain and lock our prison doors. As Max Lucado explained, "Bitterness is its own prison." We may even know joy is on the other side of these prison doors, but the roots bind us to the floor.

We refuse to forget and falsely use bitterness as a "shield" to protect us. But the truth is, we are hardening our hearts and turning away from the life of joy God desires for each of us.

We lock ourselves in hurt and pain and cover our depression with prescription opioids, internet porn, and self-isolation. Our bitterness immobilizes and paralyzes us. We inadvertently become a slave to our pain, fears, and anxieties. How long will we give these bitter roots the authority to enslave us?

Maybe it is time to let God's raindrops soften the hard, dry soil. I like how Hosea describes uprooting the bitterness in our lives, "Plant the good seeds of righteousness, and you will harvest a crop of love. Plow up the hard ground of your hearts, for now is the time to seek the Lord, that he may come and shower righteousness upon you."

When we dig up bitter roots, it literally hurts, and we don't want to "go there." We retreat to the hurt because it's just too hard. But I've come to realize, Jesus is a gentleman and an expert gardener. He won't bring in the bulldozer or excavator with brute force. His ways are kind and gentle. He patiently digs, touching the tender roots of our discouraged hearts. His scarred hands unearth these painful roots one by one. If we let Him, He has the power to expose the bitter roots, uproot them, and ultimately heal our hearts.

Forgiveness and bitterness are often linked, which is a topic we will dive deeper into in the next chapter. But before we get there, maybe it's time to call the person who has hurt us most. Or write a letter to the dad who was never there. Maybe even email the boss who fired us. Perhaps it is time to "let it go," for *Frozen* soil never produces lasting fruit.

The writer of Hebrews gives us the insight to help us excavate the bad roots. "Look after each other so that none of you fails to receive the grace of God. Watch out that no poisonous root of bitterness grows up to trouble you, corrupting many." Bitterness rots us and even plants toxic seeds to those around us.

Conversely, forgiveness delivers us to extend God's grace and joy to those we encounter every day.

Another tough, radish-type root is *anxiety.* Anxiety is an obstinate root, which quickly steals our joy. Ultimately, anxiety stems from roots of fear and worry. It breeds the unhealthy kind of fear. The keep-you-up-at night kind of worry. Our world has found quite a few things to be afraid of these days. It can be octophobia (fear of the #8), consecotaleophobia (fear of chopsticks), or the very reasonable coulrophobia (fear of clowns). These fears catapult us into anxiety, high-blood pressure, and a desire for Xanax. Please hear me out on this, for I don't want to discredit the fact that many fears are real. But our fears are also killing us. Anxiety is clouding our vision and robbing us blind. But the truth is, God didn't give us a spirit of fear or anxiety, but one of a sound mind.

Jesus knew fear and anxiety would easily creep into our lives. Perhaps it's why He spent so much time encouraging His guys not to be afraid. He knows worry steals sleep and sends us looking for a prescription to cope. I think sometimes; we need to take one slow deep breath. And then another one. Let's see anxiety, fear, and worry for what they are … the opposite of whimsy, the rival of rest, the antithesis of joy.

These different experiences are some of the reasons the Apostle Paul wrote his letter to the Philippians. This book of the Bible is probably the strongest Scriptural support of joy. Joy during times of trial and struggle. Joy in the beauty of community. Joy that liberates us from fear, anxiety, or worries. I'll let it speak for itself:

Always be filled with joy in the Lord. I will say it again.
Be filled with joy. Let everyone see that you are gentle
and kind. The Lord is coming soon. Don't worry about

anything, but pray and ask God for everything you need,
always giving thanks for what you have. And because
you belong to Christ Jesus, God's peace will stand guard
over all your thoughts and feelings. His peace can do
this far better than our human minds.

These bold statements declare this truth: living in peace and joy *is* possible through Jesus. If we let God's peace guard our thoughts and feelings; we can breathe. We can uproot anxiety. It may take some time to plow the soil. It may take some rest, tears with friends, and long walks. But it is possible. I refuse to believe we are destined to live in a whirlwind of anxiety and fear. God has a better plan. He wants *more* for us.

I think most of us can agree, bad roots are troublesome, and they taste bad. These roots are sucking our joy. Thankfully, some good, life-giving roots can be planted along the way as well!

SWEET ROOTS

As much as I despise radishes, some edible roots are delicious and even sweet. For example, the sweet potato. So good. Whether it is duck-fat fried sweet potatoes at Stock & Barrel in Knoxville, TN or my mom's marshmallow covered sweet potatoes on Thanksgiving; sweet potatoes are full of goodness. And now that I live in The South, I've been officially introduced to Sweet Potato Pie, which is a masterpiece in and of itself. This amazing root is both sweet and rich. Life-giving.

Like the fascinating tree in South Africa called the Shepherd's tree. This *boscia albitrunca* is an intriguing creation of God. The relatively small tree thrives in the hot, dry, and rocky conditions of South Africa. Often referred to as the "Tree of Life," the Shepherd Tree has a vibrant and healthy white bark, thick leathery leaves, and even produces small berries from its yellow and fragrant flower buds. It earned its nickname from the sustenance it provides to both humans and animals. How can a fruitful tree like this thrive in the dry African heat?

Roots.

Deep and healthy ones.

This Shepherd's Tree has the deepest recorded roots known to man, boasting 68 meters deep into the earth! For U.S. citizens, its 223 feet (I am still perplexed by Congress' decision to essentially abandon the metric system used throughout the rest of the world). These are some seriously deep roots. Even when the dry summer heat blasts its branches, this tree continues to produce life. Rooted deep into the soil, the Shepherd Tree is immovable. While facing toil, drought, and storm, it's still thriving with life. The depth of its healthy roots give life rather than destroy it.

The Shepherd's Tree is an excellent representation of the root of *trust*. Trusting God when life throws us a curveball is rough and perplexing. Just ask my friend Jeremy. He lost his 21-year-old wife to cancer five months after they married. The pain and sorrows were heavy. The storm raged. The tears wouldn't stop. The questions lingered like a leaking faucet. The anger welled up, and frustrations abound. This profound loss is still tangibly felt 18 years later. We all miss Melissa. She was a gem. Her smile lit up the room and her presence changed environments. You could have your eyes closed and feel a difference in the room when Melissa showed up. She made a joyful impact everywhere she went!

None of us could comprehend how this loss happened. But through it all, something kept Jeremy from shriveling up and rotting away. It wasn't him trying harder. It wasn't him going to more Bible studies or reading self-help books. He wasn't numbing the pain with food, drink, or yoga classes. It was a simple and supernatural trust planted and etched in his soul. Simply put, he trusted in the God of hope. Somehow, he found beauty in the ashes. Jeremy still can't explain any of the reasons for Melissa entering eternity at such a young and precious age.

But he *can* say, "Jesus is *trust*worthy." He still believes. He walks by faith. Trust is the root.

Growing up in northern California allowed me to experience some of the most beautiful and gigantic trees on the planet. Standing over 300 feet in height and recognized as the tallest tree in the world, the mighty Redwoods are the Daddy-O of tree swagger. Absolutely breathtaking. You really gain some perspective when driving by one of these beasts, hiking on trails canopied by its massive tree limbs, or camping near the foot of the towering red giants. You quickly realize, "I am incredibly small, and these trees are incredibly big!"

How can a tree reach such heights? You may have guessed … It's roots.

Interestingly, a Redwood's roots are only about five or six feet in depth. Yet, even with its shallow root system, the Redwood's roots are wide—often extending up to 100 feet from the trunk. These trees thrive when interlocked and even fused together with other Redwoods, providing mammoth strength against the powers of nature. The wide-bodied roots of Redwood forests offer some of the greatest beauty and sustainability known to humanity.

This type of root system illustrates *interdependency*. Notice, I did not say "dependency." A dependent, one-sided relationship is when someone solely depends on one person; ultimately, sucking some life from them. The healthier alternative is interdependency, which depicts a *mutual* reliance on one another for life. Just like a Redwood, we need each other. Mutual support from neighboring roots is essential for survival. Left alone, a Redwood Tree will become full of itself, grow top-heavy, and crash to the ground. The same happens to us when we "go it alone." Let's extend a hand, interlock with the family of God, and face life's storms together.

I think we can agree, Shepherds and Redwoods are awesome. Their roots position them for greatness and longevity. Deep, wide and intertwined with one another—they are prepared to face floods, storms, and trials of all kinds.

These are the good roots.

How *deep* with God are we willing to go? There is no limit to the depth of His love. If we want to go deep, He can go deeper still. How deep are our roots today? Are we in a spiritual drought, a heated argument, or a fire-filled test? Maybe it's time to tap into the deep root of His grace, which can not only sustain us but even produce life through us.

How *wide* are our roots in this season of life? Are we vulnerable enough to do life with others? Are we trusting each other enough to lock arms and overcome life's greatest challenges together? We cannot do this life alone. We need one another. We need the companionship and we need the family of God.

We need roots both deep and wide to experience a life of joy. Roots deep in His unconditional love, abundant grace, and supernatural peace. Roots wide in a relationship with God and man.

When the root system of our lives is healthy, joy becomes positional. Our circumstances no longer define our joy. When life punches us in the gut, we still stand. When death or disease knocks at our door, we answer with a supernatural smile on our face. When an ugly divorce cuts our heart with pain, sadness, and remorse, we find the will to live and the strength to breathe.

When debt has us backed up against the wall, the sparkle of joy refuses to fade.

Let's allow our hearts to be challenged by this scriptural statement, "Let your *roots* grow down into Him, and let your lives be built on Him. Then your faith will grow strong in the truth you were taught, and you will overflow with thankfulness."

When we are rooted in Jesus, joy becomes our testimony, our legacy, our story. Onlookers will begin to ask, "How in the world can they still smile?"

PLANTED

Planted, positioned for greatness. But can I take this ~
storm weathered against me, to be,
eternally free from death, lack of peace, I want to see ~
the blossoms take color, even as trials grow older ~
in desert winds when blowing, are You still writing my story?
Am I planted?
By streams of life and pathways of living,
bringing sounds of singing, until ears are ringing ~
with melodies of grit as I sip from lips ~
of forgiving wine, pressed through time, I am His, He is mine.
For I am planted, rooted, founded ~
in the soil, rich and clean ~ lasting fruit budding to bloom, room
of green.
Protected, positioned ...
Am I planted?
But bitterness ...
lurks within the shadows, molding meadows ~
that once glistened with brightness.
Creeping into roots, resentment brews, putrefying ointment removes ~
life from joy-filled branches, leaves and chances
to flourish in the garden of princes.
Am I planted?
Depth of love, width of an interdependent community of God & man ~
His plan to stand in war-torn land.
Rooted, planted, no longer afraid
as His roots sustain my aid ~
to both survive & thrive, multiply ~
fruit through the deeply planted root
of His unmatchable joy ...
Am I planted?
Or dying from the inside?
My roots will soon define ~
His life or mine.

CHAPTER 6

THAT DAM RIVER

Surrendering to a joyful life ...

Road trips create some interesting memories. Like when my sister Krissy and I took a long strange trip from California to Idaho. It was the summer before my senior year in high school, so I was up for just about anything. We went to visit one of my buddies who recently moved to Idaho Falls, ID and we wanted to explore the open road. Jerry Garcia had passed away about one week before we left, so in honor of him, we adorned the back window of my sister's Nissan Sentra with a sign reading, "We will miss you, Jerry!" At the time, I'm sure those who didn't follow the Grateful Dead, drove by thinking we had lost a great uncle or something.

After the long journey along the Nevada freeway, we finally arrived at my friend's house. We quickly began to plan out our time together. We decided to do some whitewater rafting along the Snake River. It was a good choice.

We arrived at the launch spot, completed the safety brief and plunged down the river with water splashing in our britches. As we bounced down the river's trail, we made memories at every turn. We even got a cool picture taken. Yet

I must ask, can you imagine if, a beaver built himself a dam in the middle of our journey and stopped our river voyage short? Even though I would have thoroughly enjoyed seeing an animal with a mullet, our joyous rafting trip would have come to a screeching halt. All because of a critter blocking us from our destination. We would not move forward because *dams block free-flowing water.*

My next rafting experience wasn't until a recent trip to Jinja, Uganda. We spent seven days in the capital city of Kampala hosting an outreach concert, visiting orphanages and working with local ministries. It was an action-packed week, full of lives being changed by the hope of Jesus. And a quick side note, Uganda is a special place. I agree with a local pastor who told me, "For some reason, the kiss of God is on Uganda." I couldn't agree more. There is a tangible, supernatural joy in this country, despite the physical, spiritual and emotional challenges they have faced as a nation.

To finish up our time and encounter the natural beauty and wonder of Uganda, we figured a Nile River whitewater rafting trip would be just the ticket. Plus, our friend Craig told us he almost drowned on his recent Nile River rafting episode. We somehow found this intriguing and thought it would be a great idea. With paddles ready, we had no idea what was in store.

Floating on the Nile River with three of my friends is now one of my all-time memories. But I'm still sore just thinking about it. With level four and five rapids, we plunged down the turbulent water with our boat guide yelling, "Forward boys!" We hit the rapids about every 15 minutes with significant airtime, whirlpools and waterfalls surrounding each drop. Adrenaline was pumping. This was legit!

After we landed the first drop like pros, we thought we were the next best rafters since sliced bread. But the mighty Nile was quick to humble us. Over the course of this six-hour journey, we had loads of fresh pineapple to snack on, and a few extra granola bars in our bellies as we finished with a 50 percent success rate of making the rapids. We were tossed and flipped out of the boat on four of the eight major drops and rapids. We came out of the day with bumps, bruises, and even a broken toe. I think each of us gulped down about a half-gallon of the Nile River. But we wouldn't trade it for the world.

As the trip concluded, our river-guide told us how the government was about to build a dam to block the last portion of the river by the end of the year. This dam will change the flow of water, thrills of rafting, and maybe even lead to the loss of some rafting guide jobs. Dams block free-flowing water. Bummer.

I recently learned how dams block over 85 percent of the world's water sources. I guess we like power and control more than we like fresh running water. Some dams are massive, like the Hoover Dam, standing over 720 feet at its crest. I remember visiting this dam on a junior high school trip to the Grand Canyon. It was remarkable to see so much water blocked by a massive brute force of concrete and steel. Whether its massive dams like ole Hoover, or small dams built by boys in their backyard during a rainstorm, both serve the same purpose. To block and preserve water. The intent for dams can be useful, as they can provide entire cities and towns with energy, hydropower, shipping facilitation, irrigation, and basic water supply. The U.S. alone has rivers flowing in and out of over 80,000 dams. It's been found more than half of these dams have no legitimate purpose other than being a national landmark. For decades, even centuries, many of these dams have blocked the fresh and free-flowing water of rivers.

These dams get me thinking a bit about our spiritual lives. We know there is a river of joy available, yet the flow of living water seems blocked and the stream is dammed. Why?

What's keeping me from experiencing a joyful narrative in life? God talks about rivers a few times in the Word, but He doesn't mention dams. You see, dams are man's and beaver's ideas. We build dams to protect and control our money and privacy. Before we know it, the rivers of joy in our lives are completely stagnant and at a stand-still.

I believe we can learn a few things from dams and rivers. We can learn about the value and beauty of *surrender*. We can all be a bit stiff-necked sometimes, put our feet down and resist the plans and purposes of God. The truth is, we think we know better than He does. Sometimes, we need to stop fighting and go with the flow. When we trust God to take care of us, and break patterns of resistance, the river of life becomes a joy-ride of whimsy, hope, and eternal purpose. Riding down the river on an inner-tube with a piña colada seems like a lot more fun than getting stuck in the mud and hanging out with beavers.

Let's look at a few *surrender points* (aka Dam Busters), which can help us eliminate the dams in our life, enjoy the ride, and even experience joy every day.

VULNERABILITY

To be completely transparent, East Africa was not the easiest overseas trip I've taken in life. I'll share some more stories about my first African experience in a couple of chapters, but I'll start with how I was hit by a Coca-Cola truck while looking at a pair of shoes on the sidewalk. To make matters worse, the driver dared to yell at *me*! I was like, "Dude, you just hit me with a delivery truck as I'm walking on the sidewalk, and you want to yell at me?" I'll never understand that one.

Yet something else happened on this mission trip, which I don't share with too many people. I still don't know if I should share this, but why not? It's part of my narrative. I was a 24-year-old single guy at the time. I wanted to make a difference in the world for Jesus. I figured going to a discipleship school at *Youth With A Mission (YWAM)* was my golden ticket to becoming a super Christian. YWAM impacts millions of lives throughout the world. And while I was confident the five-month Discipleship Training School would be epic, it also had an unexpected, eternal impact on me. It helped me know the depth of God's love for me and better understand the beauty of His voice. But God allowed a few other things to break my pride and humble me in the process.

The first three months of the program were part of the 'lecture phase.' Our school enjoyed the majestic mountains of Colorado Springs, missionary cafeteria food, work duties and classroom time learning aspects of God's character. It was a wonderful experience, yet a few internal struggles began to emerge. I, along with most 24-year-old single guys had a lot of hormones. A strong desire for companionship and an even stronger longing for sex usually accompanies this time of a guy's life. Just being honest. And harboring lust can only be hidden so long before those desires begin to express themselves in ungodly forms. If not put in check, those cravings of the flesh begin to strip a young man of his character, purpose, and worth.

I maintained a reasonable level of control and purity when I surrendered my life to Jesus, but some things began to surface while in Colorado. So, when the time came for us to board an airplane for a two-month mission trip to Kenya and Tanzania, my inner struggles took over. We made the first leg of our journey from Colorado Springs to London, UK and enjoyed some tea and crumpets in the city upon arrival. A few hours later we were back on the Kenya Airways flight for an eight-hour journey to Nairobi, Kenya. Of all places, this is where I came face to face with failure, shame, and the consequence of foolish choices. Even while writing this, I still blush with remorse.

Our team had 20 people on board, and everyone seemed to have the gift of sleep. Except for me. I was restless. Stuck in a middle seat and tired of listening to the Swedish Christian rock-band Blindside on my portable CD player. During one of my many laps down the aisle, I struck up a conversation with a female passenger from Norway who also couldn't sleep. Well, to make a long story short …

I'll save the details and put it bluntly. The conversation resulted in a make-out session in the airplane bathroom. Some may think the Mile-High Make-Out Club is a boast-worthy moment. But I just can't bring myself to agree. I was a fool and believed a lie. As my buddy, Damian said when I told him what happened, "Dude, you are a cool guy and all, but that was clearly Satan. Don't be flattered." Man, I totally blew it.

Suddenly, my sin hit me … I was on a mission trip for Jesus. I was in a discipleship training school. 19 Godly friends surrounded me. I was listening to Christian music. What in the world happened?

It was at this moment I learned some life-long lessons. First, temptation can reach us anywhere. We are not untouchable from the lures of hormones and flesh. It's better to listen to the voice of wisdom, steering us clear from potential pitfalls and unnecessary self-inflicted pains.

The second life principle I learned through this experience is just as meaningful. *Vulnerability*. I had a choice after the "make out moment" with this Norwegian stranger. I could pretend it didn't happen and hide it under the blanket of shame. Or, I could come clean and talk to someone about my poor use of time on an airplane. I chose the latter. My decision proved to be the more painful process, but I knew it was better than living a lie. With about two hours left of our flight to the hot African city of Nairobi, I woke up my team leader and confessed my blunder. He was a bit perplexed by the whole thing. With a drowsy reply, he said, "Wait. What? You did what? Dude, you have to be kidding." Then he went back to sleep.

Upon landing, he met with our other team leader in the Jomo Kenyatta Airport as we waited for our van to pick us up. I was ashamed, but I still had peace in telling him. The leaders decided I could finish out the two months in Africa but couldn't teach or preach during the outreach. I also would not graduate the discipleship school once we returned home. It was quite painful to see all my buddies receive their YWAM diploma and congratulatory hugs from homies for completing. This was my class and my community. The consequences stung, especially since I had wanted to work with YWAM since I was in fifth grade.

But I wouldn't trade the decision to confess my mistake. There is freedom in transparency. It's painful yet beautiful. We need to be an open book and not hide in the shadows.

Yet on a side note, I'm also not saying we need to go around vomiting all our sinful junk on everyone we meet either. My suggestion is to have a handful of trusted people in our lives who we can really open up with (friends, family, accountability groups, counselors, etc.). Vulnerability within a loving community enables us to receive healing support without judgment and empowers us to move forward.

My decision to be vulnerable allowed the grace of God to flood my heart and life to help me walk on the path towards redemption and healing. Amid my failure, God welcomed me into His arms, and within two years I'd meet my beautiful wife, Michelle. His mercy is unparalleled. I now know, vulnerability isn't always the easiest route, but it sure is the most valuable.

Perhaps this is why the author, speaker, and professor Dr. Brené Brown has found such an audience for her 16+ year research on the impact of vulnerability. She has discovered how joy and vulnerability are nearly inseparable.

In her TED Talk entitled *The power of vulnerability,* which has now been viewed by close to 40 million people, Dr. Brown states, "...vulnerability is the gateway to courage and joy." When we surrender to vulnerability we become free from our shame. Joy can be unleashed like a river into our daily lives.

Vulnerability is a bit scary, but if we can be honest with ourselves, transparent before God and an open book before others, the dam hindering our joy can come crashing down.

Dr. Brown even points out how joy itself takes a level of courage and bravery. Listen to what she has to say in her recent book, *Braving the Wilderness*:

It takes courage to open ourselves up to joy. In fact, as I've written in other books, I believe joy is probably the most vulnerable emotion we experience. We're afraid that if we allow ourselves to feel it, we'll get blindsided by disaster or disappointment. That's why in moments of real joy, many of us dress-rehearse tragedy.

I completely agree. We can be so filled with fear, shame, and regret that we won't even allow ourselves to experience true joy because we think punishment or travesty will blindside us. We put our reputation before the health of our hearts. We refuse to be transparent and vulnerable. But the truth is, God gives us grace even for the very thing we are most ashamed of doing. He blesses vulnerability.

This truth leads us to our next dam buster and surrender point – *forgiveness.*

FORGIVENESS

RECEIVING

When we open the Scriptures, it doesn't take long to realize we have *all* sinned and fallen short of God's purity. This means we *all* need forgiveness. We've all blown it in one way or another. We all have a sin problem. We were born with this problem, and it continues to haunt each of us every day. But there *is* a way out. Jesus came to rescue us from this problem. Romans 5:8-9 reveals the solution: *"But God showed his great love for us by sending Christ to die for us while we were still sinners. And since we have been made right in God's sight by the blood of Christ, He will certainly save us from God's condemnation."* Jesus forgives the contrite heart, gives the sinner a new soul, and hooks us up with a brand-new start.

But, when we refuse to receive His forgiveness, we add bricks to the dam, block the water, and prevent the true flow of joy in our lives.

The first step of blowing up this dam is allowing God to step in with some love dynamite to wash away our sins with one stroke of His hand. I know it's a knock to our ego, and it reveals how we just can't "fix it" alone. But receiving forgiveness from God sure does liberate us to enjoy life quite a bit more. When the wall of separation is broken down between God and us, joy is the result.

I say it's time to embrace His forgiveness.

But not just for the stuff we did before we were born again, but the crazy and stupid choices we've made after we identified ourselves as "Christians." The slip-ups, blunders, hurtful words, broken promises, fits of anger, lustful looks, road rages, or lapses of integrity. Those are often much more difficult to swallow, and the shame can load up our hearts like a pack mule.

I have two suggestions for "receiving" forgiveness. If you have never surrendered to Jesus and His offer of forgiveness, it's time. We don't have the promise of tomorrow, and His forgiveness is real, eternal and true. Just ask Him. He is waiting. And secondly, if you are a Christ Follower, blow up the dam of shame and pride. Run into His arms of grace, turn from the foolishness, and receive His unhindered forgiveness. Jesus isn't mad at you. He just misses you.

Then there is the matter of receiving forgiveness from *people* we have hurt. We have all done things to hurt other people, whether we meant to or not. Some of us have reaped havoc in the lives of those closest to us because of our pride, selfish ambition, addiction, or arrogance. It hurts even thinking about the pain we have caused. We pay major consequences for those blunders and sins. Be it divorce, estranged children, massive debt, or even prison. Sin does have a price tag.

But sin isn't the end of the story. Maybe we realized our wrong, humbled ourselves, and turned from our ways. Perhaps we reached out to those we have hurt and genuinely apologized. If that's the case, the first step is out of the way. Great!

But then …

How do we respond if they actually forgive us? Do we resist? Do we accept it? It's not always easy, but it's necessary. Wallowing in our shame will not help the matter. If someone has expressed forgiveness for the wrongs we have done, let's believe them. Joy is on the other side. And then let's ask God for the power to change and not repeat our errors. The power to learn from our mistakes and rebuild the trust we crushed. Grace is a good thing and helps pave the way to greater joy.

GIVING

Depending on the severity of the crime, misfortune, bad decision, or sin – refusing to offer forgiveness could weigh us down for a lifetime. It's understandable. Someone intentionally harmed us. We were hurt. Someone took advantage of us. They ripped our heart to shreds or stole our innocence. Being sinned against sucks. And for the record, it is not okay with God. Let me share an example ...

"The Mommy and Daddy Game." That is what they called it anyway. I recently heard this story, and it tore my heart in two. But I believe it gives us some insight into how God feels about misfortunes in our lives. A young girl was about to be launched into the mission field to serve Jesus. She wanted the elders of the church to pray for her, so she could go with a clear vision and purpose. As they began to pray for this young twenty-something-year-old girl, one of the guys began to sense a word from the Lord. "I hate mommies and daddies!" He was perplexed and thought, "There is no way I'm sharing this. Way too weird. Not going to do it!" But he couldn't shake it, and really sensed he had to tell this young girl, so he told her, "God wants you to know, 'I hate mommies and daddies!'" The girl looked at him with angst, fear, and overwhelming shame. She lost it. Screaming, weeping, raging with pain. Gut-wrenching cries from the depth of her soul. The elders just prayed and waited. Once she began to calm down, they had to find out what was going on. They eventually asked, and soon discovered the magnitude of pain she had faced in life. Family members had repeatedly molested this precious girl throughout her childhood. And they called this brutal act of incest, a game called 'Mommies and Daddies.' And God hated it. The dark perversion of this world breaks His heart. He was not okay with it. And she needed to know.

But, He still asked her to release forgiveness to those who harmed her. By no means did He excuse the sin of the perpetrators. And even though they never expressed remorse or sorrow over their evil acts, if she was to be free, she had to forgive. So, in this deep and meaningful prayer with the family of God, she released forgiveness, allowed Jesus to heal her pain, and soon went on to enter the mission field with a renewed heart. I'm certain she still walked through some counseling to deal with such pain. The deep hurts and wounds would try to surface at times. But the healing process had to start with forgiveness. Once she forgave the trespasses of others and released them to Jesus, she remained on the promised path of freedom. As Jesus said in His famous instruction on prayer, "... and forgive us our sins, as we have *forgiven those who sin against us,*" (Matthew 6:12, italics mine).

We think holding on to bitterness and rage against those who have hurt us will help make the pain go away or hurt the other person back. But it won't. Forgiveness is the only way to break this frequent dam blocking our joy.

Just ask Brandon and Jennifer ...

Brandon and his wife Jennifer have become some amazing friends of ours here in Tennessee. Their love for one another and Jesus is quite contagious. They live with raw candor, zero guile, and genuine joy. Truly some of my favorite people in this world. You'd be surprised to learn it wasn't always this way. Before their relationship with Jesus, both made incredibly harmful choices in their marriage. The choices of unfaithfulness and adultery. What some would call 'the cardinal sin.' These choices broke massive amounts of trust, inflicted mutual wounds and nearly ended their marriage. But Jesus ...

Here is the truth. When we let Jesus in, we can't move forward without *forgiveness* in the equation. Our friends soon learned the value of this painful, yet necessary process. I asked Brandon to write a quick recap of their 'forgiveness story,' so you can hear first-hand the wonder of offering forgiveness to those who have hurt you:

> Ours is a story of forgiveness. It is a testimony to the power of freely releasing someone who doesn't deserve it and hasn't earned it. It is about each of us taking responsibility. Our story is also about accepting forgiveness when it is undeserved. You see, we both committed the single most painful form of the betrayal of trust in a marriage.
>
> Our options were to either divorce and try to move on (terrible idea considering our level of brokenness) or forgive and allow Jesus to change our hearts. We decided to choose forgiveness. But without Jesus in the center, I am confident there would have been no way to stay together.
>
> That forgiveness thing can be so hard, but through the consistent decision to pray together multiple times a day, Jennifer and I decided to do the necessary work

and forgive. And by the power of the Holy Spirit, we committed not to give up. AND WOW!!

Jesus began a miraculous healing work in us, which continues today. He has shown granting forgiveness to be the most freedom giving thing we have ever experienced. Crazy as it may seem, we found freedom in doing everything the world recommends against doing. At the lowest point in our relationship, we found joy and purpose. It requires continual surrendering. It requires dependence on Jesus to take our pain and replace it with joy.

These examples show how we can unleash the river of joy in our lives through the power of forgiveness. I remember hearing someone say how the act of forgiveness can hurt worse than the pain we felt when the wound occurred. Thus, we fear forgiveness and end up allowing the pain to fester. But the problem with harboring unforgiveness is we will never find peace. I think the same is true with joy. There really is no joy without forgiveness. Let's set some explosives on the dam of unforgiveness and blow it up. It's time to let the river flow again!

DAM THOUGHTS

I have vivid memories of one of our training exercises with the U.S. Marines, as I was one of the "safety corpsmen" in the hot sandy deserts outside of Kuwait City, Kuwait back in 1998. As a 'devil-doc,' (U.S. Navy Hospital Corpsman) attached to the Marines, I was responsible for the safety of the young Marines of Bravo Company, 2nd Platoon as they shot at stuff and blew up objects to prepare for war or conflict. I only carried a 9mm pistol, but every once in a while, they would let me shoot big guns like .50 Caliber machine guns or AT-4 bazookas. It was amazing!

On this final day of training, we were asked to create our own bombs with C-4 explosives, so I packed my ammo can with scraps of metal, a toothbrush, some chapstick and maybe even a picture of an ex-girlfriend, if I'm remembering correctly. Then I put an entire stick of C-4 on top of her face. We placed this makeshift bomb about 300 yards away, lit the firing line, and watched it shake the earth and turn my ammo can into butter.

This is the kind of explosive device we need to place on the guarded and unforgiving dams. Being vulnerable with trusted friends sets the river of joy free in our hearts. And forgiveness breaks the burdens, which have been weighing us down for decades.

Let's go for it.

Plus, blowing stuff up is always fun.

BREAK

Breaking free, released to be, delivered from captivity ~
that once held hostage liberty meant for me.
Freshwater flowing, but I keep –
withholding, my heart from You. Withholding my dreams from You.
Maybe the sorrow is too great: shame holds my fate
holding heavy weights ~
of pride & isolation, fear & trepidation, masked with false
expectations ...
Hidden shames. Who is to blame?
Is it me or the name ~ of the one, two, or three
who inflicted wounds to hurt me.
Release these ...
Burdens block the stream it seems, but everlasting water brings ~
life to the dying, freedom from lying, multiplying –
wonders of grace covered blunders.
Making beauty from vulnerability ~ providing tranquility
to the exhausted builder of these dams.
Break the sorrow, break the silence
heal my tomorrow, I surrender in reverence ~
to Your presence of deliverance from this dam of unknown
ignorance.
Because freedom sings ~ the song of surrendered melodies ...
Breaking the dam, voice of the Lamb
calling out the son of Adam, this man – I AM
your River, your delight – I AM
your song in the night – I AM
your water, your life ...
I respond ~
Break the broken places that bind me

Cookbooks

Scene 2

I know everyone may think "their mom" makes the best lasagna in the world, but my mom really does. And she isn't even Italian! I don't know how she makes such a magical dish, but I do know she uses some key secret ingredients. And now, my mom has passed on the recipe to my wife. Oh, snap oh la! The recipe must include a little bit of this and a little bit of that, or it just doesn't taste right ... The "wow" factor is missing. The same is true for living a joyful narrative. Walking in a life of joy isn't possible without the secret sauce. Let's explore some simple, yet necessary ingredients for joy.

CHAPTER 7

HAVE YOU SEEN MY KEYS?

The magical tools used to unlock doors ...

I'm grumpy. A lot. Just ask my wife. Almost weekly, Michelle challenges me and asks, "Where did Danny go? Where is the joyful life you love to talk about?" "Where are the bubbles? Where is the 11th Commandment guy?" (The unofficial 11th Commandment is *"Thou shall not sweat it!"*, the classic motto of my Dad growing up). Why the frown, why the fear, why the frumps? Do I really need to be a cantankerous drab when things don't go my way? Why does worry deem necessary when facing change or challenge? I need to ask myself, "Where *is* my joy?"

Joy doesn't run out. It doesn't have to be a faded memory. Joy is always present and available for the child of God.

I often forget this.

Maybe you can relate.

We get wound up in our little worlds and bear the brunt of our fears and worries. It's effortless for anxiety to cloud our vision. One look at my news app and headlines of sadness abound. Or when I open my bank account and see funds depleting again, I feel stress sweep into my life. I go down bunny trails of anxiety. The blood pressure rises. The sleep fades. Concerns pile up. I don't have as many Instagram followers as Jeremy or Bob. My back hurts, I ate another donut, and I have a lingering headache. My kids are sick again. Crap. Here I am, writing a book about joy and I haven't belly laughed with my wife in more than three months. I haven't told my boys a good story in weeks.

Heart check.

My joy is missing.

Kind of like losing a set of keys.

At some point, we all have experienced the case of the missing keys. "Where did I leave them?" "When did I last have them?" "Honey, have you seen my keys?"

During my early days in San Diego as I was learning to surf, I made a serious party foul, which probably ruined a guy's day or week. As I was stretching and zipping up my wetsuit, I noticed a set of keys stashed near the rocks. They were carefully placed safe from crashing waves and supposedly hidden from thieves. Being a true novice at the time, I failed to observe Rule #91 of surfing etiquette, which is, "Don't move or touch a hidden set of keys near the beach." So, I, being the kind, young fella I was, grabbed the keys. I moved them to a totally different area of the beach, far away from the rocks, waves, people, and paths of men. In other words, far from where the owner might find them. Oops!! As I paddled out to face the giants, this poor surfer was about to come in from a surf session and begin a distressed search for his missing keys. Time to call the locksmith for the car, house, office, and who knows what else. I'm so sorry, bro!

Keys hold a high priority in our lives. We use them to open doors. Or start our cars. And even to access treasure or a safe in the closet. Without keys – doors remain closed, the car stays parked, and the treasure lays dormant. Stress and frustration set in when we are "locked out" and can't get in without breaking a window or calling a tow-truck.

I think the same is true with joy.

We all know it is there, but it feels like we are locked out. We begin our search thinking "it's got to be somewhere." Joy is something we all long to experience. Seriously, have you ever met someone who wants to be miserable and depressed? Even goths and Marilyn Manson fans want to experience joy on some level. They may look in unusual places to find it, but they want it.

So, I wonder, what will unlock the door to a joyful and abundant life?

Here is the mojo. Here are the master keys ... You can't unlock the door to lasting joy if the keys of *love* and *obedience* aren't on your keychain.

Let's look at this from a "Talladega Nights" point of view – *love* triggers the spark plugs and sets the pistons in motion, while *obedience* pumps pure refined oil throughout the engine to keep things running. I don't know much about NASCAR or Formula 1, but I do know you need these basic things in a car to win a race. The same is true with joy.

Jesus gave a promise of joy to His followers, but it came with a set of keys. Those keys can't be tucked away in a purse, stowed in the overhead bin of an airplane, or lost in the laundry basket. They are not behind a rock at the beach. The love and obedience keys are meant to be used in this Christian life to unlock the abundant and joyful life Jesus promised us.

DON'T CRY FOR ME ARGENTINA

I have vivid memories of our two and a half years spent in the South American country of Argentina. We lived in the bustling city of Mar del Plata, which was one of the few beach cities in the country. Our house was about 11 blocks from the ocean, making sand a standard household item. The boys thrive with Vitamin D, as does my Pacific-Islander wife. Winters in Mar del Plata were cold and windy, but summer was an entirely different story.

The hot summer days beamed with bright sunshine, bustling coastlines, beach umbrellas, cookouts with Argentine beef on the parilla (Argentina-style grill), and giggly kiddos splashing in the waves. Michelle loved these times. She delighted in watching our boys at play and pondering the deeper blessings in life. But when she looked over at her husband expecting to see mutual amusement, she'd find the untouchable Mr. Frump. Self-absorption, navel-gazing and confusing depression overwhelmed my first season of church-planting. Depression was something I hadn't dealt with since my early teenage years, so having these old emotions of melancholia and worry was quite uncanny for my heart and mind. I even traveled down roads of suicidal thought and contemplated ways of escape. It was weird, dark and troubling. Daydreaming about offing myself was unfortunately common during this season. The spiritual warfare was real, and my emotional state was spastic.

Even though our time in Argentina included some tough moments, I wouldn't trade it for anything. We have some amazing memories and made lifetime friends throughout those 895 days. I'll always have a deep and genuine love for the people of Argentina. But man, I went through a massive spiritual wilderness. I was preoccupied with my missionary success (or lack thereof) and my internal struggles with fear, insecurity, and depression. I began to bypass the joys of everyday life. My constant sense of inadequacy disrupted the simplicity of life's greatest gifts.

People. Family. Joy.

When my sister came to visit, she immediately saw through the fluff and called me out, saying, "Danny, you are cold. I've never seen this before. What's up?"

I simply didn't have an answer. I just knew I needed a breakthrough.

I still remember sitting across from her at our dining table with her big ole green eyes of fire wanting to see her brother whole again. She challenged me to get some counsel, work out whatever marital issues we had and tap into the well of joy again. The conversation was heartfelt and real. I'm so thankful for the candid conversations and sincere love she always sends my way. Side note, we need people in our life to call out our BS occasionally. It hurts, but it works. Let's listen to those who love us enough to tell us how it is and help us see our blind spots.

By the grace of God, I slowly weathered through this wild wilderness season. I discovered how the joy I longed for never actually left. I just lost my keys. They were there all along, but neglected and unused.

After some time, the keys of love and obedience began poking through my man-purse. I was desperate for joy. It was time to dig through the junk and look under the couch of fear and insecurity. My love key grew dull from ignoring the sweetness of my wife and kids, and from missing God's constant, massive love for me. My obedience key was rusty, as I discounted promptings of the Spirit and Jesus' gentle whisper. I decided to do some heart searching, mixed with repentance and surrender. Before I knew it, the keys were washed off, polished up and ready to open the door to joy.

Jesus' promise of joy is evident in John 15:11, as He declares, "These things I have spoken to you, that my joy may be in you, and that your joy may be full." He wants us to know and experience *His* joy to the fullest measure.

Look closer at His declaration, *"These things* I have spoken to you ..." What are "these things?*"* The two verses before His statement explain it well. "As the Father has loved me, so have I loved you. *Abide in my love.* If you *keep my commandments,* you will abide in my love, just as I have kept my Father's commandments and abide in His love."

The combo to the master lock and the basic math equation:

Love + Obedience = Joy.

It's time to unlock the door.

Abiding in His love is pretty simple. Love God. Love people. Be loved by God. Be loved by people. Henry Blackaby explained the value of God loving us as he said, "To be loved by God is the highest relationship, the highest achievement, and the highest position in life." Let God love you. He loves you more than you can imagine. And Bob Goff gives a simple way to love others, "While you're figuring out what God wants you to do next — go love everybody."

And keeping His commandments merely is about saying "yes" to Jesus. It's worth it. There is a supernatural, unexplainable joy that seems to pair with obedience. When we are obedient to His promptings, joy is the result. I like how D.L. Moody combined joy with obedience by saying, "The Lord gives His people perpetual joy when they walk in obedience to him."

In the following couple of chapters, we will talk a bit about the keys of love and obedience. They are difference makers. They unlock doors. Joy is available on the other side.

UNLOCK

Unlock. Open. I long to find You again,
Friend of sinners bend your ear,
Calm my fears – to remind me You never left me alone,
Your gentle whisper calls me home to joy once known ...
Knocking, but I'm fumbling, dropping, looking ~
Wondering if I'll still be pondering desperation
On the front steps of a joy-filled house.
Stare through windows, occasional stained glass ~
This just can't last, for the past still haunts the present,
While pride manipulates the remnant ~
Of unspoken opportunities to walk inside ...
Tear-stained struggle with pain, self-inflicted wounds the same,
You call my name –
With love.
Never letting me drift into sifting seas of inward depression, for
this lesson –
Gives no counterfeit key to open doors of joyous meaning.
The other side – greener grass, softer meadows & peaceful
streams ~
Songs that last, flowered petals, sunshine daydreams.
The gate breaks from hinges when ears open to Your speech,
As You teach, my soul will reach, beginning to breach
The wall that lies between us,
And enter –
the pasture my heart longs for.

CHAPTER 8

LOVE LESSONS FROM MT. KILIMANJARO

*The 'power of love' is more than a Huey Lewis or Celine
Dion song...*

I was in the second month of a team mission trip in Kenya and
Tanzania in late 2002, and let's just say it was not the smoothest
experience of my life. I mentioned the Coca-Cola truck and
airplane incident already, but these were not the only challenges.
In just six weeks, I had already been stolen from three times. One
thief jacked my portable cd player. Another snagged my wallet as
I was trying to get on a bus. And the last swindler was the best of
all. He reached through a bus window and snaked my camera right
off my lap. As he sprinted away, our bus driver jumped out his
driver's side window and started to chase the guy! No joke. So, I
had to follow suit, along with every other tough North American
boy on the bus. A pack of us sprinted after this bandit. Dude, he
was fast. We dashed through one small village across the highway
as onlookers cheered us on. Then he made a sharp right turn into a
cornfield with our fastest guy about 50 meters from him.

"Get him!" we yelled.

The hunt for Mr. Fox went on for another half mile or so
until he reached an entirely different village. It was crazy. By

this time, I began to hear the theme song from *Rocky II* because I looked back to see about 100 little Tanzanian kids trailing us trying to capture the guy ... all for my camera. I felt so loved.

But we never found him.

Our labor was totally in vain.

At least I got to high-five a bunch of curious children and make some new friends.

Unfortunately, the trials didn't stop there; I also contracted malaria. I developed some fevers and experienced the worst stomach cramps known to man. If you have never had malaria, maybe I can give you a visual. The stomach cramps compare to the feeling you get when you overdose on ice cream, and all you want to do is suck your thumb and hug your mommy. It's pretty rough. And I had the mildest form. Making matters worse, was the whole malaria "testing" process, but I'll save it for another time. All I'll say for now is it did involve the bathroom laboratory.

The last straw was the two-week torture of passing a kidney stone. It all began in the middle of the night, and I thought my kidneys were falling out. I remember kneeling by my team leader's bunk-bed, hoping he remembered my mom's name in case he had to notify her of my death. It was nuts. Waves of nausea, some vomiting, and repentance consumed the rest of my night. I thought I was about to meet Jesus at the age of 24. But grace pulled me through, and before I knew it I was face to face with a local doctor. His response to all my agony was a bit surprising. "Ha!" he laughed. "You, my friend, are passing a kidney stone. Drink more water. Hahahaha!" Was this actually happening? I just faced death, and Dr. Giggles is laughing at me. The next 14 days, five hours, and eight minutes were horrible. Since we were out in the bush-bush, the only way to pass the sucker was through pounding glasses of boiled H2O tasting like burnt rice, charcoal, and a hint of ash. No laser therapies. No shock treatments. There wasn't even cranberry juice or olive oil to help it flush out. Sheesh. Yet, I'll never forget the day it passed. We were about to take a five-hour bus ride across African plains, and I was dreading the journey. But before we took off, the urge to pee shot into my bladder like a rocket and the only opportunity to "go" was outside on a brick wall. That baby of crystallized pain gave birth on the base of a cement block with me shouting joys of "Hallelujah! It's a boy!" I know having a baby is much more radical, but I can honestly say I can relate. Just a little bit.

THE UPPER ROOM

Africa was harsh on ole Danny Boy. Through all this, I also learned that a strong dose of legalism was creeping into my faith. I had been walking with Jesus for about seven years and had a sincere zeal for Him, but I was missing the point. As I sought to be the next great missionary like Hudson Taylor or William Carey, I became consumed with a relentless pursuit of trying to earn the favor of Jesus. But during my many evangelistic and international endeavors, I forgot the pure and sweet love of God.

I was quick to point the finger at others and their shortcomings. I was accustomed to rebuking friends, internally criticizing their weaknesses and being extremely hard on myself in the meantime. But something happened during one night of worship in a small upper room in Dar el Salaam, Tanzania.

It changed me forever.

There was about 18 of us having a team bible study followed with some worship songs. Things went as usual, with some cool songs and passionate prayers from my team members. The songs were being belted out, and we all were having a good time with

Jesus. Then, I began to sense God's gentle hand, and loving voice grab my attention. It was one of those holy moments when you know something deep and profound is about to happen.

His loving whisper nudged my heart.

"Danny, stop trying to impress me ... I already love you."

Whoa. Those words hit me right in my core and touched the center of my soul. Jesus stopped me in my tracks. The tears flowed. His truth was beginning to set me free. Within a short amount of time, I was curled up on the floor in the fetal position with buckets of salty tears and snot bubbles. It was at this point my buddy and team leader John, touched my shoulder, and spoke a prophetic word from Jesus, *"I love you, I love you, I love you, I love you, I love you ... "* Again, and again Jesus reminded me of His everlasting love. Not because of anything I have done, or said, or accomplished, but just because I am His. He loves me. He loves me. He loves me. This simple truth rocked my world and I've never been the same.

Let Him love you. Let Him enjoy you for who He created you to be. We don't need to impress Him to gain girl-scout cookies or little league trophies. Hang out in His unshakeable love. Jesus said, "Abide in my love." He likes you, delights in you, enjoys you, and smiles when He sees you. Soak it up, friend. His love is real and true. If we stop running and let Him love us, it can transform everything. It changes how we view Him, it changes how we perceive others, and it changes how we see the world. Abiding in His love is the first turn of the key to encountering a life of joy. That hot African night, I allowed His love to grab hold of me. I began to see others with a greater sense of grace. I started to enjoy life a bit more. I smiled and laughed more. The reality of Romans 8:38-39 took root:

And I am convinced that nothing can ever separate us from God's love. Neither death nor life, neither angels nor demons, neither our fears for today nor our worries about tomorrow—not even the powers of hell can separate us from God's love. No power in the sky above or in the earth below—indeed, nothing in all creation will ever be able to separate us from the love of God that is revealed in Christ Jesus our Lord.

His love makes all the difference. The more we embrace the love of Jesus, the more present the joy of God becomes. As I will say a few times, *joy is responding to the greatness of Jesus.* And this joy can only be unlocked with His key of love.

You can find thousands of books about God's love. Love is the very foundation of our Christian faith. "For God so *loved* the world …" "God *is* love." He is the very definition of love, the example of love, and the essence of love. C.S. Lewis provides insight into the type of love God bestows on His creation:

God is love, 'Herein is love, not that we loved God but that he loved us' (1 John 4:10). We must not begin with mysticism, with the creature's love for God, or with the wonderful foretastes of the fruition of God vouchsafed to some in their earthly life. We begin at the real beginning, with love as the Divine energy. This primal love is Gift-love. In God, there is no hunger that needs to be filled, only plenteousness that desires to give.

By nature, God is a Giver. His love is powerful, matchless and the ultimate gift to us. He gives out His love to all who would receive it in the Person of Jesus Christ, His only Begotten. All He expects in return is for us to receive it and allow our lives to be absorbed by it.

HGTV

I'll always remember receiving the key to our first home. It was a big deal for us. After all, we spent the first 12 years of our marriage gallivanting around the world. We had always been renters. If something broke, we called the landlord. If we wanted to move, we would fulfill our lease and move along. But when we moved to Tennessee, we knew it was time to plant some roots. Homes in the Nashville area were a bit more affordable than California, so if the right house came on the market at a reasonable price, we would pull the trigger. Thankfully, we soon found a great neighborhood with a double cul-de-sac, super friendly neighbors, and Fourth of July block-parties with a bicycle parade and cherry bombs. It was just the fit we needed to take the plunge into homeownership. So, after we settled all the legalities, formalities, and technicalities, we signed the dotted line. With a bright blue pen. We made the initial payments and became homeowners. All I had to do was hold out my hand, and someone placed the key into my shaking palm. We found a new life. Memories are now being created with my wife as we enjoy the Tennessee evenings in our Cracker Barrel rocking chairs, watching our kids at play. We are abiding in our home because we have the key to every door in the house.

I think the same is true with this key of love designed by God. The key is in the shape of a cross. Yep. You got it. Jesus' love opens the door! His sacrificial death on those bloody, wooden beams made salvation available for you and me. His death was the essence of love on display. And His matchless resurrection became the Rose Bowl Parade of God's mighty love. Not even death can hold back His love for you! Stretch out your trembling palm and feel His nail-scarred hands give you the key to His house. Love opens the door, and HIS JOY stands at the threshold.

Let's ask some important questions mentioned by Henri Nouwen about our soul's love life as we wrap up this chapter:

Did I offer peace today? Did I bring a smile to someone's face? Did I say words of healing? Did I let go of my anger and resentment? Did I forgive? Did I love? These are the real questions. I must trust that the little bit of love that I sow now will bear many fruits, here in this world and the life to come.

One of those fruits He speaks of is joy. Joy today and joy in the eternal. Did I love today? Did I receive God's love today? Let's keep an eye on those love keys. Joy is waiting.

LOVE

Now this is a bit difficult, for the subject can be so broad ~
Some love to embrace, staring upon the face
Of a beautiful queen, or remaining unseen
Behind the scenes, knowing their offerings are seen
By the One who loves them ~ deeply, eternally, monumentally
Displayed upon a cross so cold to make story unfold of lasting
love so bold,
to be told ~ through ages in song, melody, poem and truth ...
Breakthrough, move ~
This unbelieving soul to a place of worth
More valuable than rubies, proposing chance at new birth ~
This is love ...
We mix up this overused word with romantic honeymoons and bliss,
How we have missed ~ the majestic kiss ~ From heaven to this –
Place of loneliness ...
Love is a word used to write expressions of devotion ~
A potion making motion in the bloodstreams of children
Longing for belonging in a family of grace ~
Bring me to the place ~ where this word is real,
Placing a seal of matchless beauty
Upon these stained hands in need of cleansing, I'm repenting ...
For your love is remaining
And reminding me of ~
Unbelievable joy ...

CHAPTER 9

FOLLOW THE PROMPTINGS

Listening to God is easier than we think ...

It was the second night on my first ever three-day fast. My walk with Jesus had just taken a turn onto Passion Avenue, and Jesus led my Dad and me to a time of fasting and prayer. We were going for it. Just water. No Otter Pops or peanut butter smoothies. By noon on day one, my stomach began to eat itself, and hunger struck. But we persevered and refused to give up. Jesus had led us to this, and we wanted to follow. By the second night, my tummy sounded like a bear lost in the woods, and I could not sleep a wink. So, I did all I knew to do during a restless night with the urge to pee every 10 minutes, and a sincere desire to hear from God ...

Pray.

Having a chat with Jesus seemed like the thing to do. I was pretty green in my faith, so I prayed away without expecting Him to respond. Well, He did.

In the middle of the prayer session, I suddenly felt like I needed to take a walk. Ummm. It was 2 a.m. in a small town in Northern California. Taking a walk in the middle of the night came with an expectancy to hear squirrels rustling or see twinkling stars shining above my head. Since I wasn't planning to eat a bowl of cereal or make some toast, I decided to follow this prompting and go for a stroll. As I began to walk down the quiet street, I saw a man about 200 yards away heading towards the only nearby store open 24 hours a day. But I didn't think much of it and continued my saunter down the street. But then came the gentle nudge again. Go to *Jackpot*.

Jackpot? This was the store I went to for Scooby snacks and Kiwi-Strawberry Snapple. Why would I go there? I couldn't buy anything besides a bottle of water, so I was curious why I felt a nudge to go. But ok. I couldn't shake the gentle prompting, so I listened and walked on down to this overpriced gas station and convenience store.

When I arrived, I saw a distraught man sitting on the curb near the store's entrance. It was apparent he was in pain. I figured I would ask if he was ok.

"Dude, are you cool bro? Are you in trouble or pain?" I said.

"I'm hurting!" he mumbled. "I recently developed a crazy tooth infection, and the doctor told me if it persists, it could lead to my brain and cause major complications. I'm scared, bro. But I can't afford to call an ambulance."

All this was before the cell-phone era, so I had to come up with a plan to help this homie out. "I know, I can run home and get my truck to give this guy a ride to the Emergency Room!" I thought to myself. Cool, I'm going to do something helpful.

At the very moment the notion popped into my mind, my long-time buddy Mark Z. pulled into the store parking lot in his dirty pickup truck. Mark was a great guy and always a good bud to have around. He was rocking the tie-dye t-shirt, smoking his Camel Lights and jamming out to The String Cheese Incident as he pulled up to the curb. I was like, "Bro, what are you doing here? It's like two in the morning?" I think he had just run out of beer or something so he was probably loading up for a night-cap. But regardless, he was there. Right when I needed him. The timing was spectacular.

He was just as surprised as I was. I had left the once familiar party scene, so he probably was even more perplexed as to why I would be hanging out at *Jackpot* at 2 a.m.

He had a quick reply, "Dude, what are *you* doing here?"

Mark and I gave each other a bro-hug, and I jumped right to the point. "Dude, see that guy over there? He totally needs to go to the hospital! He has some weird tooth issue, and it's about to hit his brain!" Mark immediately raced me up to my house to grab my truck, so I could transport this guy to the Emergency Room.

Within four minutes, I was back at the store, and my newfound buddy hopped in the vehicle as we sped away to the hospital. During this rushed trip to the ER, I was even able to hear a quick bit of his story, share the Gospel with him and give him a small Gideon New Testament. I would never see him again, but I had a front row seat to God's amazing love for one soul! I also learned a lesson about gentle promptings that night. We are encouraged to follow all promptings of the Holy Spirit. In other words, obey Jesus. If we are being led to do something righteous, worthwhile, meaningful and helpful, we should go for it. Leave the results up to God. Obeying His loving voice and responding to His Word brings some interesting excitement. It may even bring some joy.

Simple *obedience* is the second key to unlock a storehouse to the joy of God. Once again, Jesus said so. If we obey him and keep his commandments (loving God and loving people), we abide in His love. When we are willing to live out our faith and obey the gentle, holy promptings of God's Spirit, a wide door of joy flings open.

Life gets pretty joyful when we are willing to obey. As my good friend, Charlie Campbell once told me, "There is no joy without holiness." How true this is. Yes, there are moments of pleasure and happiness this world experiences. Our society is chasing hard after such indulgences. But the problem with these pursuits is how they only offer short-lived enjoyment and are absent of God's lasting pleasure. When we abide in His love with a heart of sincere obedience, we welcome His Holy Spirit to the party. Lasting joy can fill the room. My friend Charlie said it. Jesus said it.

The "key" of obedience is a treasured gift the Lord has given His kids. He has entrusted us with the freedom of choice and desires our uncomplicated obedience. You can bet love, wisdom, and strength are the foundation of His promptings. It's as simple as saying "yes" to Him.

As with a lot of authors, I also like to quote Timothy Keller. He writes some awesome stuff. I love how he summed up obedience by stating, "The essence of Christian obedience is not do's and don'ts but personal allegiance to Jesus." Keller also brings up the direct correlation obedience has with joy in his New York Times best-selling book *The Reason for God,* which states:

> Yes, he does ask us to obey him unconditionally, to glorify, praise, and center our lives around him. But now, I hope, you finally see why he does that. He wants our joy! He has infinite happiness not through self-centeredness, but through self-giving, other-centered love. And the only way we, who have been created in his image, can have this same joy, is if we center our entire lives around him instead of ourselves.

Trusting in His selfless love and righteous promptings can lead us into *His* abundant and joyful life. Are you willing? Am I? Let's grab ahold of this valuable key and explore where a life of obedience will take us!

God has been trying to get the attention of humanity for years with this one. His encouragement for obedience started in the Garden of Eden with Adam and Eve, carried over into the history of Israel, and now rings true in the lifeline of the Church. Blessings are found in obedience. The choice to enjoy those blessings are up to us, as God declares, "Today I have given you the choice between life and death, between blessings and curses. Now I call on heaven and earth to witness the choice you make. Oh, that you would choose life so that you and your descendants might live!"

You and I can choose life. Let's love God, obey Him and commit ourselves to Him. The *key* to excitement in life is found in a simple choice to obey Jesus.

COSTA RICA

Let's consider my friend Phil for a moment. I met my good buddy around 20 years ago on a Navy vessel headed for the Persian Gulf. Phil was a true United States Marine (USMC). Some think he works for the Russians though because he looks a lot like Ivan Drago from *Rocky IV.* To this day, Phil carries an exceptional level of intensity and commitment in all he does. Once a Marine, always a Marine.

I was a Navy Hospital Corpsman, serving on the "green side" (attached to the USMC), giving me the privilege of standing alongside the finest and the fittest in the U.S. Military. We had set sail on the *U.S.S. Denver* with the intention of possible war with Saddam Hussein. We all seemed to have this sense of fear, excitement, and patriotism running through our veins. There I was, standing on the bow of the ship one evening. During those days, I was usually talking to God about girls, wondering if the girl I was crushing on was going to be "the one." I soon realized I wasn't the only guy who talked to Jesus about the ladies.

That is because when I looked over to my left, a blonde-headed Marine was standing nearby. This bro really did look like Ivan Drago! I thought he had to be undercover for the KGB (once the spy and state-security of the Soviet Union), but I soon found out he was doing the same thing I was ... having a chat with God about a girl. Phil was a great bro from the start, and we immediately hit it off. By God's grace, we have remained great friends ever since. We have experienced some of life's greatest moments together. We stood by each other's sides on our wedding days when our wives walked down the aisle. We are watching each other's kids grow up. We have sipped on countless cups of coffee together, and now we have the tradition to spend Thanksgivings together as families. Our best memories are from when we have seen each other take leaps of faith to obey Jesus.

Seeing Phil respond to a simple prompting of the Holy Spirit proved to be life-changing for me. And now, countless others. After the military, at 22-years-old, Phil went to work at a church in San Diego. He has been in ministry ever since, and it's been awesome to see God call him to paths of faith and obedience.

For example, when he was a college pastor leading a night of worship and Bible study, Phil heard the Lord speak to his heart in such a clear and precise manner.

In this quiet moment, Phil sensed the Holy Spirit say, "Go – Costa Rica!"

That's it. No more, no less.

You know what Phil did? He responded to the prompting.

I saw it first hand as we boarded the airplane together in San Diego alongside his wife Rebecca, and their 10-month-old daughter, Eden. Phil obeyed God, and hundreds of lives were affected as a result, including his own. He and his family served Jesus faithfully in Tamarindo, Costa Rica for close to 10 years. During this time, they planted a church, launched children programs and developed leaders. People surrendered their lives to Jesus, and the on-looking world saw a simple young man obey the Living God. He even surfed some amazing waves and seemed to learn Spanish in about 15 minutes.

The result of Phil's obedience–JOY.

Yes, all the fruit of Phil's service was due to God's grace, but this simple step of obedience opened a portal of everlasting joy.

So, let us entertain such lifestyles of trust and obedience.

I say we give it a shot and take some risks.

Let's listen to the Holy Spirit. Let's respond to life-giving Scriptures.

Let's follow the promptings and enter the life we were created to enjoy!

LISTEN

So eager to talk, I miss the chance to listen ...
Or quick to walk – away from two-way conversations, regarding
sensations
In the heart and eardrum – I need some –
Time to think this through.
Listen. Listen.
You really want to say something,
Even while I'm changing the direction of my affections
Which has a way of reflecting the inward subjection
I've given to lies and distraction ~
from the truth, since the days of my youth, wearing the suit –
Of falsehood, masking the roots which contribute ~
To my reasoning for plugging my ears to all You have to speak ...
Listen. Listen.
A gentle tap on the shoulder, a delicate song in the night –
Why would I fight the right to sight,
and sound of holy communication?
Where will this lead – this divine opportunity to
Believe abundantly in the life you promise me ...
Listen. Listen.
To the eternal prompting, always inviting, never condemning yet
always convicting –
Me of what I know to do – Or not do – It's true
If we would only ...
Listen. Listen.

A Never-Ending Story

Scene 3

One of my absolute favorite movies as a kid was *The Never-Ending Story*, as it provided me a mutual love for both books and movies. Imagination unfolds, and characters come to life. The boy in the movie wasn't just reading about the plot and storyline. He was beginning to live in the story. The same is true with this idea of our lives becoming a Joyful Narrative. We don't have to view joy from the outside looking in. We can experience joy and live in joy through every chapter, scene, and moment of our existence. And I believe you realize by now, joy is far more than just being 'happy' all the time. Remember, living in lasting joy is simply responding to the reality of Jesus. When we acknowledge God in our midst, we welcome joy in humor and heartache, sacrifice and silliness, triumph and tragedy. It is a beautiful and never-ending story …

CHAPTER 10

FIVE-YEAR-OLD'S CAN'T DRIVE

Humor and his friends

Joe Banks. What an interesting guy. When I think of him, I get an instant picture of his one-of-a-kind beard, belly, and chubby fingers. He was my Dad's friend and came over quite a bit for shish-kabobs, root beer, and to play music with my Pops. He and his wife, Pam had a couple of kids who we hung with when their parents visited.

My fondest memory of Joe was when I was about five-years-old. I think we were helping them move, but I'm not sure. Either way, I was sitting in the driver's seat of Joe's big, white van, which was parked about 20 feet away from their front porch. Now, if you have ever seen *A-Team,* it was the same type of van Mr. T would drive, except white. As I pretended to race around the block, Joe handed me the keys and asked me to back the van closer to the house. I thought, "Dude, are you serious? I'm five! But since you asked, OK!" He explained how to fire up the engine and rev it a bit. Looking good so far. I could barely touch the petal, but I was eager to drive this puppy. He stood next to the driver's window and coached me on tapping the petal and backing it up slowly. "Alright, I got it. I'm ready, Joe!"

As soon as Joe reached in and shifted the van into reverse, I slammed my foot on the gas. The *A-Team* van shot back like a rocket, ran over Joe's right foot, and continued up to their front porch. I was amazed! Joe wasn't as amused. The van broke his foot, his porch, and most of all, his pride. Homeboy let a five-year-old drive his van! The hilarious truth in this is basic – five-year-old kids can't drive, bro. But man, what a story.

These humorous moments must crack God up a bit. Those stand-out memories can even pave our path and shift how we see the world. Sometimes those random acts of stupidity or silly mishaps bruise our egos or break our feet, but God knows; eventually, we will look back fondly with belly-aching laughter. In my opinion, these moments are some of the richest treasures in life.

SIGN MY FACE

I've never been into the ritual of getting autographs from celebrities or well-known public figures. And up until my early twenties, I still didn't understand why authors signed their books. I now know it helps authors strengthen connections with readers, but during those years, I was clueless.

One Sunday evening, my buddy Damian and I headed to a service at a large church in San Diego. We arrived early and spotted a young man asking for the lead pastor's signature. I thought, "Bro, why is he signing autographs before church? I know he used to be a professional athlete and all but come on!"

Now the thing about my friend Damian is he is full of wisdom, and incredibly crafty when it comes to practical jokes. Thus, he decided to play along with my ignorance. As he handed me a pen, he asked, "Dude, why don't you go get his autograph? Wouldn't that be hilarious?"

I decided to take it up a notch, and replied, "Yeah man, I'll ask him to sign my face." Damian was all over it and dared me to give it a shot. True story. I'm always up for a challenge, so I grabbed his writing implement and walked up to the front of the church. I boldly handed the pastor my pen, and asked with an audacious grin, "Hi Pastor Miles! Will you sign my face?" What in the world was I thinking? Imagine if he said yes! I would be walking around the church with a permanent autograph from Pastor Miles McPherson on my forehead and cheek. Thank Jesus he gave me a confused look and kindly replied, "Ummm. I have to go," and took off backstage. I looked back to see Damian in tears from laughing so hard. Oh man! What a memory. We still laugh about it to this day.

You see, humor helps us 'not take ourselves so seriously.' Seriously, I'm serious. We tend to orbit our worlds around our problems, egos, and stresses—radically hindering humor. But when we allow some righteous laughter in, it's harder for pride to take us down a path God never intended us to go down. Let's start seeing embarrassing moments as opportunities for hilarity and comedy. Maybe our pride will take a hit, but if I had to choose between laughter and stress ... I'd choose laughter every time.

SPAGHETTI DINNER

I was one stoked eighth grader rocking my hip-hop overall shorts and a hyper color t-shirt. I was just invited over to my new girlfriend's parent's house for a spaghetti dinner. They wanted to get to know the guy crushing on their daughter. Her dad's name was Bob, and he was a large man with strawberry blonde hair and an interesting personality. Her mom's name was Patty, and she was nice and held manners as a high priority in the home. Especially at the dinner table. I was also raised with a good sense of manners, proper napkin placement, and lived by a general rule to be clean and tidy at the dinner table. I felt ready to make a solid first impression on this girl's family, so that I could take her to the upcoming school dance. I loved school dances because I could do the 'roger rabbit' and the 'snake' super good. Actually, I still can. Especially when they play Vanilla Ice.

Anyway, before dinner, the conversation was flowing, and my confidence was soaring. I was making my new girlfriend's parents smile, and her little sister thought I was super hip. A most triumphant time. Then it was time to enjoy the spaghetti dinner Patty prepared. She set out the whole shebang. Salad, garlic bread, and some supernatural sauce to top the noodles. I politely chowed down on my dinner as we all talked. But the magic marinara began to put some pressure on my stomach. Oh no. I squeezed the cheeks as hard as I could, but to no avail. Next thing I know, the sound of a dying mouse making a high-pitched tune off the base of my chair came out of my derriere! It happened so fast, and there was no turning back. Oh, snap. I just cut the cheese at the dinner table! And it was at *her house!* My face turned the color of the spaghetti sauce. But, Bob. He came to the rescue. Less than two seconds after the gas pass, he blamed it on his youngest daughter. "Krissy! What was that?" he said. "I didn't do it, I promise!" said this precious 10-year-old girl. I played along with the family, and blamed little Krissy for slicing some queso at the dinner table! By golly, it worked! I never came clean with the truth about me being 'the one' who did it.

I guess this is my confession 26 years later. I haven't talked to the family in a couple of decades. But if you are reading this now; just know, it wasn't Krissy. Danny cut the squeaker. ☺

Memories like these keep my heart soft. They keep me from my tendency to be a Debby Downer. I can't wallow in a depressive state when I remember these moments. Humor is like a vitamin boost to our joy supply. Laughter is medicine. Humor is a gift.

I BELIEVE IN SCIENCE

Smile. It works. It heals.

I believe and support the science of smiling. A smile can have a powerful impact on our bodies and souls. Did you know that the positive health effects of laughter can last up to 24 hours? The American Heart Association also found laughter and smiling to reduce artery inflammation, diminish stress hormones and increase HDL cholesterol (the good kind). The Proverbs were right after all as Solomon penned, "A cheerful heart is good medicine, but a broken spirit saps a person's strength."

Children have us beat on their ability to crack a smile. In fact, on average, children smile about 400 times per day, while adults can barely manage 20 grins within a 24-hour period. Amazing. Let's take a few notes from the kiddos and go for 30 smiles in a day, or maybe even 100 ...

Smiling even makes a difference in marketing, business, and sales. A drastic one. An article in the *Journal of Consumer Marketing* supports this logic, as the case study concluded:

Our main finding was that marketing objects (ads and packaging) comprising pictures of a smiling model produce more positive attitudes toward the objects than pictures of non-smiling models. We also found that smiling models in this context induced more consumer joy, suggesting that the effects on the attitudes were a function of affect infusion. In addition, our findings indicate that both emotional contagion and typicality mechanisms contributed to consumer joy, and that attention factors seem to have played a negligible role.

Wow. Even smiling models have a more positive and joyful impact on customers, consumers, and clients! Smiling is powerful science indeed. I think we should squeeze out some more smiles every day. It may even save someone's life.

Growing up just outside the bay area of San Francisco, means I've strolled the Golden Gate Bridge a time or two. I love walking across this beautiful bridge with the cool bay area breeze upon my face, the views of the city and mysterious Alcatraz down below. And even with its beauty, the Golden Gate Bridge has become associated with numerous calamities. In fact, an estimated 1,250+ people have jumped off the bridge to their deaths. And if someone simply smiled, there may have been one less tragedy at the Golden Gate Bridge.

A young man jumped off the Golden Gate Bridge on a windy afternoon to end his life. The morning before his suicide, this young man wrote a short note on a piece of paper. It said, "If one person smiles at me today, I won't jump."

He jumped.

This story wrecks my emotions every time I think about it. Why couldn't someone just smile? Where was his family? Did he have any friends? I'll never know the answers to these questions but one thing is sure—he isolated himself. Even if he had family or roommates, he detached his emotions, fears, and life from others. Nobody knew he just needed someone to smile at him.

COMMUNITY

But if there is so much blessing and joy even in a single encounter of brother with brother, how inexhaustible are the riches that open up for those who by God's will are privileged to live in the daily fellowship of life with other Christians!
~ Dietrich Bonhoeffer

Think about it. How many times have we enjoyed belly-aching laughter – alone? How often have we giggled, snorted, or lost our bubbles without someone by our side? And even in those rare moments when we crack up while rocking the solo, doesn't it usually involve other people? Watching a funny movie by ourselves includes other people (the actors, the plot, etc.). Laughing alone from happy memories even involves other people. Fond memories with friends and family, which produced so much laughter represented one important thing. Community.

Humor, laughter, and joy are nearly impossible to experience without the collective of people. We need each other. We need each smile. We need each chuckle. We can't do it alone. Some isolation is good for a breather or to recharge. But clamming up and dwelling alone over long periods of time can be dangerous and even tragic. It becomes easy for lies to creep in when we isolate. Seclusion buries our joy. Like the Proverb states, "He who [willfully] separates himself [from God and man] seeks his own desire, he quarrels against all sound wisdom."

Bottom line, we miss out on joy when we isolate ourselves from other people.

Isolation and loneliness can even plague our physical health. Substantial evidence reveals how individuals who lack community and connection (both objective and subjective social isolation) are at higher risk for premature mortality. The dangers associated with social isolation and loneliness are comparable to other risk factors for mortality (physical activity, obesity, substance abuse, responsible sexual behavior, mental health, injury and violence, environmental quality, immunization, and access to healthcare). Trying to do life without community can shorten our lives. We literally *need* friends.

One of my favorite movies of all time is *It's A Wonderful Life*. I think I have seen it at least 39 times because I've watched it every Christmas Eve since birth. There is a reason this 1946 film moves my Dad and me to tears every year. It's because life is a gift, and the connections we have with people make all the difference. The angel Clarence leaves George Bailey a note at the end of the movie to capture the power of friendship, "Remember <u>no</u> man is a failure who has <u>friends</u>." Friends are the most significant contribution to humor and laughter. Friends are the bread and butter of life. If we avoid human connection, we can't experience the joy God desires to give us. And I'm not saying we need to all be extroverts, busybodies, or chatterboxes. But *do life* with the people God gives us. Cry together. Eat together. Laugh together.

INDIAN TRAINS AND PITTING EDEMA

One of my best friends in this entire world is a bald man named Mark Schneider. We've been buddies since 2001. And even though we often live about 3,000 miles from each other, we remain connected in brotherhood. In our nearly 20 years of friendship, I can honestly say every conversation we have includes laughter. It is true. We've been the best man in each other's weddings, our kids are close in age, our wives are buddies, and when visiting San Diego, their house is the first we visit. He is the best listener I've ever met, and I thank God for this man.

Our friendship began from a mutual desire to go to India and share the love of Jesus with the 1.3 billion who live there. We planned our first trip in 2002 with a visit to Bishop Atma Ram, the dad of my YWAM buddy Jeshu. Atma's vision was to see teams from the U.S. come to serve Jesus, preach the Gospel, and work with the local churches. Mark and I wanted to go for it.

Our long journey began with a 28-hour Air India flight. Upon landing, we took a train from Mumbai to Bangalore for 24 more hours. We were picked up from the train station in Bangalore, hopped on the back of some motorcycles and soon arrived at Atma's house. And who would open the door? The Bishop's daughter, Joy. And what a gem! This girl was so incredible that Mark married her two years later! Great name. Great girl. My buddy scored.

This month-long trip bonded us for life and stirred us to launch a nonprofit ministry together. It was a massive turning point in both our lives to see the needs before our eyes, the different types of smells every 100 feet, and the overwhelming hospitality of the Indian culture. It was hot. Nasty hot. Bus rides were sticky. Sleeping on mats was uncomfortable. Food was spicy enough to make us sweat. I developed a weird condition in my feet because of the travel and heat called pitting edema. It was super gross. Some Indian ladies even stopped me after church one day to rub coconut oil all over my toes. We ate so much rice, curry and Indian biryani one night I almost stopped breathing. But man, we laughed. A lot. We bonded. And such laughter would be absent if I went alone. Ask Mark. He went back alone for a few months. No late nights of uncontrollable laughter. Just him and his uncomfortable sleeping mat. To enjoy life to the fullest, we need one of humor's best friends – community. From the start, my friendship with Mark showed me how much community impacts our joy. When we embrace community, it allows us and others to experience God's immovable, supernatural joy.

BROS

Many friendships have radically impacted my life. If I write another book someday, maybe I'll do a chapter on the amazing friends God has given me. For example, I'll probably have a chapter called *Jordan*. Because some of the most amazing people I've ever met are named Jordan (You guys know who you are). But with that said, I couldn't write about community without mentioning some of my lifetime buddies: Damian, Jeremy, Phil, and Jason. These guys are examples of the friendships we all need.

Damian. Now a chaplain in the Navy, Damian is one of the wisest and most intelligent people I've ever known. He is a genuine soul with perfect candor and a laugh that is contagious and sincere. Humor threads his personality and character, joy radiates from his life, and his love for Jesus runs deep. I know whenever I call him, he is there.

Jeremy. He makes you feel like your best friends after spending 20 seconds with him. I've been fortunate enough to have him as a friend for 20 years. He is exceptionally gifted in all he does, be it music, business, or sports, but keeps it real and is humble. His passion for Christ is incredibly infectious, and his life has impacted millions.

Phil. Always on a mission but never taking himself so seriously that he can't laugh at his blunders. If Phil is your friend, you have a friend for life. He is incredibly loyal, encouraging, and gifted. I love this guy. And he was the state wrestling champ in Nevada two years in a row so don't mess with him. His four kids and loving wife Rebecca reflect the wonder of his loving leadership.

Jason. This fuzzy ball of love is the best Bible teacher I've ever met. Seriously, homeboy can bring it. His intuitive personality, high intelligence, and devotion to Jesus keep us all on our toes. Don't try to beat this guy at golf either. His golf game is on point. Love this guy's unwavering commitment to his call of ministry. Unparalleled and holy grit.

No matter where we are in the world, we are connected. Laughter permeates our conversations and joy radiates through both good times and bad. Joy and humor are nearly impossible without the gift of friendship. As Charles Swindoll said, "I cannot even imagine where I would be today if it not for that handful of friends who have given me a heart full of joy. Let's face it; friends make life a lot more fun." So true. Plus, it sucks to be lonely. Let's be friendly. Let people into our lives. Let's embrace community.

CO-PILOTS

Marriage is the heart of true community, intimacy, and the supernatural bond between two human beings. The man, the woman. Two different creatures with the capacity for a joyful connection beyond words. I agree with the book title *Men Are Like Waffles – Women Are Like Spaghetti*, as we are just so incredibly different. Guys and girls don't just look different; our brains are contrastive. Our emotional needs tend to be opposite. But these differences are the magic of it all. The friendship between a husband and wife is like butter. It's the secret ingredient we need to make everything taste better.

It's why I consider my wife Michelle, my best friend. She is God's gift to me, and we get to do life together. We are called to laugh together and cry together. Her beautiful smile fills the room and is the cream to my coffee. Her love for laughter, practical jokes, and incredible whit are just a few of the reasons I love her. She keeps me from taking myself too seriously and reminds me of the joy found in quality time. Her listening ear is consistent, and her amity runs deep. I totally scored!

Michelle and I have had our bumps, trials, and mistakes. But we are grateful to have each other for these long days, and short years. Maintaining friendship in our marriage is the essential ingredient if we are going to make it. It's worth pursuing. It takes some trust, vulnerability and a boatload of grace, but it is possible. We don't just have to be roommates with benefits. We can be friends too!

GRATITUDE

I don't have to chase extraordinary moments to find happiness – it's right in front of me if I'm paying attention and practicing gratitude.

~ Brené Brown

A thankful heart is a joyful heart. Joy and gratitude go together like peas and carrots, french fries and ketchup, spaghetti and meatballs. If you think about it, humor is nearly absent when we are not thankful. Can we genuinely laugh when complaining about not getting our way or lusting after our neighbor's new car? Are tears of joy running down our cheeks when we worry about what our classmates think, or what our co-workers say behind our backs? Nope. We slam the door on joy and laughter when we are preoccupied with other people's opinions or weighed down with covetousness.

We must be *grateful* to experience joy. It's why my favorite American holiday is Thanksgiving. I love Christmas, Easter and The Fourth of July too. But Thanksgiving, in my opinion, is the holiday for a real awakening to joy. It's not just about the immense calories we will likely consume. It's about the friends and family who travel many miles to sit around a table with loved ones, eat a feast, and be thankful for life. I love it. And I love my mom's pumpkin pie, gravy, mashed potatoes, green bean casserole, biscuits ... you get my point.

This amazing holiday leads me to a thought about being grateful for food. This is why I'm a big fan of sincere, but *short* prayers before eating. Is someone truly thankful for food when they take 10 minutes to pray for it? It makes me wonder. Now, if you want to have a prayer meeting, do it. But not right before we eat. Just saying …

I hope my children can learn the beauty of gratitude. Gratefulness contributes to the laughter and joy we all desire. I hope I can be more thankful. Even in the valleys and deserts of life. When life is just tough, which it is often, am I still grateful for the sunset, the base of the waterfall, the apples growing on the tree? Am I willing to pause and be thankful for the blooming orange poppies growing wild on the hillside during heartache? I hope so.

Let's open the window and let the breeze of humor, laughter, smiles, community, and gratitude into our homes and hearts.

MEDICINE

Once sick with sadness, a light of smile brings gladness,
A remembrance, a deliverance
From the bonds of sorrow or worries of tomorrow
Maybe I'll borrow a grin from You?
For blue skies start to peak through, all things new
Each mercy filling morning ... Telling story upon story,
Laughter reflecting glory;
Stop. Take a sip ~
Of this medicine – starting to chuckle again,
Amongst circles of friends, from beginning to end,
As light-hearted burden lifters connect with communities
Of beauty.
Free from hostilities of insecurities, I can be me with this remedy...
Let me not underestimate the fate of those who taste ~
These healing waters of liberation, exaltation
Of the One who created the dance of romance
With humor and joy, for this boy
Who longs to laugh alongside the Friend of sinners, the Giver ~
Of new beginnings, sounds of singing now ringing
With child-like giggling ...
This ... is Medicine ~
Humor, a blessing. Laughter, a gift. So let me sift
Past the mire of confusion, break the illusion that I'm
Not to enjoy –
Life.
For today is the day of play-filled devotion with
One who never stops loving me.

CHAPTER 11

AMERICA'S MOST WANTED

The testimony of His presence ...

L ife. What a gift.
But sometimes, it's just so hard.

UNCLE SPIKE

The phone call we hope never to receive. An early morning ring awoke my dad from slumber into a living nightmare. My grandparents' neighbor was calling to let him know the Ukiah Police Department needed the nearest kin of Mike Williamson, his younger brother. The house had been on fire, and there was a dead body on the scene. With a trembling hand, my dad held the phone, wondering if this was really happening.

What? I need to come to the house to identify a body? There was a fire? There is a crime scene? Why? How?

Oh no. Not Spike! Not my brother, my friend. The one whose life was just radically transformed by Jesus. The one who was set free from drug and alcohol addiction. How could this be?

On August 1, 2000, a 19-year-old drug-induced man, named Jared Hernandez murdered my Uncle Mike ("Spike"). My uncle was house-sitting for my grandparents for a few days, attending weekly AA/NA (Alcoholics Anonymous/Narcotics Anonymous) meetings and putting up the fight to stay sober and love Jesus. My uncle participated in these meetings to help others find hope and freedom from drug-dependency. He had a passion for seeing people break the chains of addiction, which had ruined his marriage and family years earlier.

Mike's life was really turning around. He was clean and sober from heroin, alcohol, and meth for the past 20 months. He was learning to love again and was in continual fellowship with other believers. He was restoring relationships. For the first time in 42 years, he told his parents he loved them. He and my dad became friends again. He began to read Scripture. There was even talk of healing in his marriage. I really loved this guy! My uncle was brilliant and had a fascinating love for world history, golf, and coffee. Chats with him were always unique, as we sipped on espresso and discussed history or life's perplexities. He referred to my dad as Duck, so I naturally became "Little Duck." He was my Uncle Spike.

Nobody could confirm the motive of the murderer Hernandez. But he broke into the house around 2 a.m., killed my uncle with an aluminum baseball bat during his sleep, robbed the home of my grandmother's jewelry, and tried to light the house on fire. Our family wept. Our questions lingered through blinding tears. How could this happen?

The case would remain open for the next 13 years.

The mystery even appeared on "America's Most Wanted" on two separate occasions.

Somehow, the FBI tracked Hernandez down in Ensenada, Mexico more than a decade after the crime. After years of uncertainty, heartache, and questions, justice prevailed.

Hernandez received a life sentence, and our family gained a sense of closure. My dad expressed forgiveness from the stand and challenged Hernandez to surrender his life to Christ. Even with some closure, the multi-year process took a toll on my family. Especially my dad and my grandparents. Losing a brother. Losing a son. Words just can't describe the emotions associated with such pain. But amid this loss, I saw something supernatural in both my dad and my grandma.

Joy.

Seriously, my grandma and my dad are some of the most joyful people this world has ever known. It's their legacy. I want to give some attention to my Grandma Maggie. She was a gem. Just months after they sentenced her son's killer, she would breathe her last breath and enter the arms of Jesus. Here is a bit more of her story.

My Grandma Maggie's years were full and abundant. Her testimony was the ongoing, never-give-up kind of joy. Everyone who met her came face-to-face with kindness, genuine concern and unconditional love. But this love of hers, and this supernatural joy was tested time and time again. Whether it was surviving the trials of breast cancer, open heart surgery, or the loss of a son, her circumstances said anything but joy.

Yet, her joy remained steadfast.

She still smiled. She still loved. She still laughed. She still had peace. She still had joy. Yes, she cried. She had fears and sorrow. She had frustrations. She had sleepless nights. But her joy was unwavering.

During a visit to her house, I had a moment in time with her I will never forget. She had a spot on the couch where she liked to sit and read her Bible, journal down thoughts, and talk to God. I remember plopping down on the couch next to her one afternoon. I wanted to try and discover a few things about life. I guess I was somewhat baffled by her ability to smile and laugh even when she faced so much adversity and pain. I just couldn't wrap my mind around it.

So, I asked, "Grandma, how do you still have joy in the midst of all this? I mean, you recently had open heart surgery, you survived cancer, you weathered the storm of a son's drug addiction, watched the redemption in his life and then had to lose him to a tragic murder. How can you still smile?"

She paused. Tears welled up. Lips quivered a bit. Silence.

Then she replied with a simple, yet profound answer. "*I know Jesus is there*. He is with me in pain. He is with me in the sorrow." I just rested my head on her shoulder, trying to let her words sink in.

I know Jesus is there.

This is what I call *painful joy*. The supernatural joy found only in the presence of suffering. Indescribable grief. The kind of anguish where silence is medicine and the quiet presence of a friend is our only comfort. Tears become food, sleep becomes infrequent, and the pain doesn't leave. The nights of weeping weigh heavy, and the tears just won't dry up. It feels like we can't breathe. Gasping for hope. Gasping for air. Gasping for life.

It is here, in this place, we have an opportunity to see the strength of joy in its most raw and vulnerable expression. To look not only for hopes of mountain-tops but to see the blossoming flowers in the valley. To witness the Gardener carefully tending to His delicate and fragile plants. To see Him walking in the valley with us. To feel His shoulder catching our tears. He is the Intercessor, the One who dared to proclaim, "… be sure of this: I am with you always, even to the end of the age."

Just knowing "He is there," like my Grandma Maggie said, is sometimes the only resolution we have. His presence is enough.

The presence of a Friend who is closer than a brother. He carries us through the storm to walk us into the morning's sunrise.

OWEN IVES

I remember sitting alongside my wife in the hospital after the birth of our third son, Josiah. Smiles and celebration permeated that second week of September. One of those smiles was from one of my wife's besties, Darlene. Dar is one of the most wonderful people Michelle, and I have ever known, and her husband Nick is the cream of the crop.

Dar came to meet Josiah, give us some snacks, and pass out some squishy hugs. It's always a pleasure to see her, and it was extra special for her to visit. But this time, she not only came with some snacks and squishes, but she also shared the news that she was "on the nest," pregnant with her and Nick's first child. Double-rainbow-type celebration in the hospital room that day, to know Dar and Nick were soon to join the parent club.

But things don't always turn out the way we hope.

Pregnancy was rough for Dar, and about 20 weeks later, Darlene and Nick would spend the next 2 ½ years in the hospital alongside their precious baby boy, Owen Ives. Due to various complications, Owen arrived 16 weeks early in January 2015. Their road has been long. They have an incredible journey of *painful joy*. Darlene wrote this on their family's blog less than a month after Owen was born on Feb 20, 2015. The emotional roller coaster, the questions, the fears, the … I will let Dar explain.

The Waiting Game
You may see us smile, laugh, or carry on. And when you ask how we are doing, we may respond, "Hanging in there." It's a response that's not either good or bad,

but deep with the realities of our world right now. You may think we are strong or full of hope and faith. And yes, I hope that's the case because that's how we want to be, full of faith and strength.

But the truth is there have been all too many nights and days when I sink in tears and doubt. The thoughts of "will this horrible roller coaster ever end?" "Will we ever be a normal family?" "Will Owen be ok? Will he make it?" The thoughts and downward spirals are always present. The ups and downs of Owen's day are constant realities that he is still very sick even though he's making progress. The reality is that we still have a long way to go. And a way to go to not give up. To have hope and faith. To continue believing we will take him home one day soon. It's hard. It's all relentless. And it sucks.

This perfectly beautiful and sweet little baby entered our world way too soon. And now we get to see him grow in ways most people don't, but amid all the beauty of having this precious life in our world is the grief of wishing he was still in my belly. The grief of knowing he is struggling through life way too early. The grief of watching the doctors and nurses do all they can and feeling at times helpless to make him better. I want to see him better. Not tomorrow. Not in a few weeks or months or even years. I want to see this beautiful, tiny, innocent boy better now. No more hurting. No more pain. No more struggle.

And gosh, isn't that the heart of God for us? He sees all we go through. He sees us. And His heart is to make us better. Whole. And isn't that what we look forward to on the other side of this life? No more pain. No more struggle. I cannot wait for that. To be totally and completely healed ... mentally, physically, emotionally, spiritually ... healed. And for all things to be made right, and to experience that with so many but mostly with God. Oh, I can't wait. There, Owen will be totally and completely well. One day, hopefully far, far down the road from now. He'll run and leap and be totally free.

But here we are, in the here and now. Forced to live in the present. Forced to stay in the waiting. So ... we wait. Wait for Owen to grow and us to go home. Wait for the peace in the midst of the ups and downs. The peace that God promises when our minds are focused on Him. Wait for the day Owen is more stable. Until then, I wait and wait with hope. Wait for God's timing in all this. I'm not saying it's easy, but I am saying it's a must. Our life depends on it, now, and always.

We have watched, prayed, cried, and hoped with our dear friends on this journey. It has not been easy. But Owen is a true fighter. Days, months, years of tubes, surgeries, tracheotomies, G-tubes, and I.V.'s ... Somehow though, there are supernatural smiles on the faces of Nick, Darlene, and now little Owen. They have chosen to agree with author Margaret Feinberg, who states, "The biggest myth about joy is that it only flourishes in good times, or that it is only the byproduct of positive experiences ... Life's thorniest paths can lead to great joy." They have embraced this thorny path of their story with hope. With joy.

Whenever we are back in San Diego, we spend some time with them, even if it's five minutes. And every time, we are overwhelmed by the beauty of this family. Their joy is unwavering. Jesus has never left little Owen, and He has never left Dar and Nick.

That's how He rolls.

And it's why we can bank on His joy being part of our story, just as the Abrams family does each day. If we simply trust Him in the storm, we may even see the blossoming rose in the valley.

Let's fast forward to present day and see the faithfulness of God in Owen's life. He still has some tubes, a tracheotomy, and a grip of medicine routines. But this little buddy has not given up the fight. On October 11, 2017, Nick and Dar were finally able to bring their boy home from the hospital. A true celebration!

But – they are still in the valley. Has the workload of caring for him become easier? Nope. Have their doctor appointments stopped? Nope. Do they ever grow weary, tired or afraid? Yep. Do they still wonder what the future holds? Yep.

But the joy of God doesn't leave their home.

I asked Dar to send me a short paragraph about how things are today. I also asked her to talk about how they still embrace joy three years later. I hope she writes a book about this one day. As you can see, home-girl can bring some rhetoric to the table!

April 2018

For us, joy didn't come in a flash because we willed it. For us, joy was this beautiful spiritual recipe of time spent with God and choosing hope every day. But the hope wasn't in our circumstances. Hoping everything would get better. Hoping we could go home and get back to life as usual. The hope was anchored deep behind the veil ... it was anchored in eternity. Hope was anchored in Him who *is* our hope. So, the joy was not tethered to our life circumstances or even anything about this life. Our joy didn't mean happiness. Our joy was tethered to our God of hope. Our hope that no matter what may come in this life, we get Jesus after. We all get wholeness after. And that hope caused a joy that left us free of fear of "what happens next?" Not that we didn't have to battle for it. We chose to walk in it. Because living in joy meant living in life. Not death. And for us, our only option in that time of our lives was either joy and life ... or depression and death. Not all stories end with a happy ending ... and ours is still being written, but for now, our life's call will be to choose hope. Choose God.

Joy means walking in "life." Embracing life and hope in the valley. Their joyful narrative has proven this to be true.

We count it an honor to walk alongside Nick, Dar, and Owen. They are a treasure to this earth. I try to have a routine with my boys when I tuck them in at night. I ask them to pick one person to pray for each night. So often, it's Owen. Maybe you would like to join my boys and pray for Owen today. I hope so! Here is a link to their never-ending story of joy: http://owenives.tumblr.com

With both the loss of my Uncle Spike and the testimony of little Owen, the case remains the same. Recognizing the simple; yet, majestic presence of God makes all the difference. The joy found in pain. The joy found amid suffering. The joy in knowing He is there through it all.

The Psalmist nailed it when he said, "You will show me the path of life; *in Your presence is* fullness of joy; at Your right hand are pleasures forevermore." This truth is our shoulder to cry on, the pillow to catch our tears, the blanket to comfort our broken and weary hearts. Jesus promises His joy will *remain,* and that His joy will be *full*. This means His joy can be present in the process, the people, and in the pain. Because He is there, joy is there. In His presence is the fullness of joy we long for in our lives. Let's look at one more story of painful joy before we move on ... it's a story of how God's love pursues us no matter where we are.

UNDERGROUND HEROS

A few years back I got to visit China and South Korea with my good friends Jordan and Nate. I had a window seat on the 13-hour, nonstop trip from Los Angeles to Seoul, Korea. Jordan slept the whole flight, and a 4-foot-10-inch lady insisted on the aisle seat. Climbing over the two of them every hour for bladder breaks wasn't the best flight of my life. But regardless of the less than ideal travel situation, it was a fantastic trip.

We bounced around a few cities throughout China like Kunming, Guangzhou, Beijing, and the Hainan island. We taught at underground Bible colleges and visited some of the most committed and brave Christians I have ever met. We held four-hour teaching sessions where the students were crammed into a room, sitting on small stools, eagerly listening to the teaching of the Bible. It was remarkable to hear them sing songs of devotion, pray with fervency, prepare to share the love of Jesus, and maybe even plant some churches. When I told my boy Isaac (who was three-years-old at the time) about our travels and adventures in secret Bible colleges in China, he quickly coined us "Underground Heroes." But truth be told, these young students were the real underground heroes.

After our time in China ended, we pushed our way into South Korea to visit some of Jordan's friends. One of those friends was a young man by the name of Samuel Lamb. He took the term "underground hero" to another level. We learned how he was a refugee from North Korea who escaped the communist stronghold just years prior. Samuel grew up seeing tragedy and experiencing pain beyond belief. Friends hanging on gallows for speaking against their leader Kim Jong-Il (father of present-day North Korean leader, Kim Jong-un), families dying of starvation and a complete unawareness of God's love and hope.

Even at a young age, Samuel knew there had to be a better way. For months, he would scout the guards, watching their every move, and timing their transitions. Finally, at the tender age of 18, in broad daylight around 2 p.m., Samuel made a break for it. While the guards were changing shifts, he quietly climbed into the Yalu River and swam across to the shores of the North China border. He made it unnoticed. He proceeded to China and began looking for work, food, and shelter.

Fear, worry, hunger, and pain filled the next three years. His first 24 months in China were spent working as a slave/shepherd in a local village with meager wages and a hungry belly. Once again, he knew he had to escape. Finally, at 21-years-old, Samuel found a way out of China. Slipping on board a train, then a boat, then a car, he made his way into Cambodia. He spent close to six months in a small house, planning for another escape. He had to get to the safe-haven of South Korea. But it took another six months in Vietnam, hoping for shelter and food before he was found and given refugee status in Seoul, South Korea. Still, he had no idea of God's love. His suffering was plenty, and his troubles refused to go away. But as Francis Thompson once noted, God is the "Hound of Heaven." He never stops pursuing us, His love for us endures, and He longs for our company. It is true for you and me. It was true for Samuel Lamb.

Upon his entry into South Korea, Samuel found a small apartment, an opportunity for university education, work, and a roommate. His roommate was a young international businessman from the United States. This foreigner had a sincere love for Jesus. And for people. The love Samuel watched, the words of truth he heard, and the simple lifestyle of this young 'Christian' quickly exposed him to the Gospel. This businessman soon led Samuel to a relationship with God through Jesus Christ. Despite all his suffering, all his heartache and loss, all his paths of running for freedom, Samuel was finally free. His soul was free. His heart was alive.

By the time we met Samuel, he was walking in this newfound internal freedom with Jesus and was already planning his path back into North Korea. "What? You want to go back!" I asked. You see, Samuel is a true "underground hero." He can't bear the thought of his friends, family, and countrymen in North Korea never hearing about the saving grace of Jesus. He had to go back. He was willing to go through whatever pain was necessary to do so. This too is *painful joy*. The joy of bringing hope to others, no matter the cost. No matter the pain.

Like the two young Moravian men, John Leonard Dober and David Nitschman. One a potter, the other a carpenter. Boarding a Dutch slave ship off the harbor of Copenhagen bound for the Danish West Indies on October 8, 1732. Both these young men had promising futures in their fields of work, were brilliant communicators, and influential in their communities. But they could not ignore their love for souls, fueled by a love for their Savior. They boarded this ship with no return ticket, willing to sell themselves into the suffering of slavery to reach the slaves of the West Indies. They stepped aboard this ship with a sense of *painful joy*. They were willing to lay aside dreams of marrying a wife someday and raising a family. They relinquished the comforts of their home for an indigenous living. They set aside pleasurable joy for painful joy.

As the vessel was untied from the docks, slipping into the open sea, the two men stood tall from the stern and shouted,

"May the Lamb that was slain receive the reward of his suffering!"

They could say this because they knew they didn't go alone.

Jesus sailed with them. His joy went along for the ride.

What is most amazing about this story is that the work of the Moravians in this region of the West Indies would carry on for another 50 years, with an estimated 13,000 people placing their faith in Jesus from their efforts!

Their *painful joy* was certainly not useless.

IT HURTS

I can't breathe, heart on my sleeve,
Isn't there some kind of reprieve?
I believe.
But I don't see ~
Anything but pain, shame, blame ~ stains
Mark the pages of this narrative with tears,
My fears steer hurts that ~
Just won't leave ...
How did this happen, how did I get here?
Why the suffering still year after year ~ of
Questions, concerns, aching that burns like ~
Fire. But You gently whisper "child,"
I am close –
To the broken with love and devotion, blood in motion
Making beauty from ash heaps,
Joy in the mourning. Life in your valleys.
Never alone. I am your home ~ of
Safety & simplicity, strength & security, peace and tranquility –
Come to Me.
I am gentle. I am kind. I am yours. You are mine.
I know your hurt, but you will find ~
Painful joy to employ
The hope this world longs for ...

CHAPTER 12

NUNS & BASKETBALL

Realizing it is not 'all about me.'

BEATRICE

On a recent trip to Uganda, the first leg of my journey was a short trip from Nashville to Boston. I planned to brave the 5-degree weather during my long layover to catch up with a buddy. I was geared up to read some Brené Brown, tackle some journal entries, and put on my noise-canceling earphones to shut out the world before I met up with my bro. But everything changed when a couple with a crying baby kicked a nun out of her seat for more leg room. Since she did what every nun is expected to do, she gave up her spot and took a seat next to me. When she sat down, she said, "How bad would that have looked if I said no?" I was immediately intrigued by this nun's spunkiness.

I had to take off the earphones. I mean, when do we ever get the chance to sit down next to a nun for 2 ½ hours? So, the questions started rolling, and I soon discovered Sister Beatrice quickly lived up to the meaning of her name. Up until this flight, I didn't know the name Beatrice means "she who brings joy."

Oh, snap! I'm sitting next to "the joy giver!" And this sister loved Jesus.

Initially, I was surprised how open and transparent she was with me as I dropped questions like, "What led you to become a nun?" and "How do you find joy?" or "What are some of the challenges?" The truth is, she is a person just like you and me. A real, robed, heart-pumping human being who has feelings, emotions, highs, lows, struggles, and pains.

She happily answered my questions and shared one of the greatest challenges of her commitment. She said sometimes people expect Sister Act or The Sound of Music to blaze out of her windpipes. Some stare, expecting nuns to be somber and still wherever they go. Think about it, what do you imagine a group of nuns to be doing at the airport? Exactly. She knows. But she and her buddies have a lot of grace on us common folk. She knows her habit garbs, and cool headband throws some people. The more we talked, the more I saw these little sparkles of joy in her eyes and smile. If you think about it, she does have a pretty radical, faithful, and loving husband – Jesus Christ. He is a way better husband than I am. I think my wife would agree.

As I ate my airplane pretzels and sipped on ginger ale, Beatrice shared some of her life experiences with me. Like how challenging it was to see the only man she would ever marry just one week before her final vow to become a nun. And he was still single. Talk about a test. But she knew this is what God called her to, and she was ready to give her life and service to God and others. She also shared when she first sensed the call to become a nun. It was during a visit to a Convent as a college student, which moved her soul. As Beatrice observed these nuns in their daily routines, she realized they had something she didn't. It was so moving that she walked away from this gathering of sisters frustrated by the joy, peace, and simplicity they expressed in life. Can't we all relate to longing for the joy we see in someone else? When someone has a special spark of love, peace, and joy, it makes us a bit uncomfortable. Maybe it's because they have something, we don't.

Beatrice couldn't shake it or ignore it anymore and had to explore her options. She knew God was calling her to something unique. Something sacrificial yet satisfying. Something deep yet simple. After a few more visits to the Convent, some long talks with God and her family, she finally concluded, "I'm called to be a nun." Woah! I sure am glad God didn't call me to be a monk. But at the same time, as I talked to Beatrice, I realized this woman has so much life to give. She's discovered the beauty and joy of a selfless life.

Her mission in life is to *give*. Beatrice currently serves alongside other nuns at a Convent in Ireland. Together, they help the local community, give to the poor and are a beacon of light with each step. She still has lonely days. She still misses family. But she has found treasure, which no man or society can provide. The gift of giving.

To others.

To God.

Those 2½ hours sitting next to Beatrice helped me rediscover the truth that my life is not just about me. And the sooner I embrace that, the sooner I experience the joy found in selfless living. It really is better to give than to receive. I forget this on a continual basis, especially at Christmas time. Or on my birthday. But the life and story of Sister Beatrice reminded me how beautiful it is to give.

The early 20th-century poet Kahlil Gibran discovered this treasure when he said, "I slept, and I dreamed that life is all joy. I woke, and I saw that life is all service. I served, and I saw that service is joy."

Service is joy. I get to give. I get to serve. I get to share.

My biological sister, Krissy, also reminds me of the beauty of giving. Because Krissy loves, I mean loves, giving gifts. She usually asks me what I want for my birthday about eight months in advance. Whether it's hiding my Christmas gift in the washing machine, mailing our family a living room size beanbag with our last name embroidered on it, or sending my boys and me an inflatable dinosaur outfit, my sister loves to give gifts. The joy Krissy experiences in giving far outweighs the pleasure of receiving a gift from her little brother. It's a beautiful thing!

Life is too short to live just for me. Other people need me. Other people need you. But I wonder if we are just too busy to give. Too preoccupied to notice others' needs. Too stressed to stop and help that lady change her tire in the parking lot. Am I so wrapped up in my world that I've stopped dating my wife? Am I accessible to our three little boys who want to talk about Avengers, Legos, or the best basketball player of all time? Am I available for the early morning phone call from a friend who needs some encouragement? The truth is, when we give a listening ear or offer help, we experience joy.

Since we are on this subject of selflessness, I can't help but mention Bob Goff. If you are like the other million people who have enjoyed his books, you probably know why Bob is someone who emulates pure selflessness. I mean, the guy puts his cell phone number in the back of all his books. Who does that? It's both awesome and inspiring. The guy made himself radically available to love people. I recently learned he plans his annual calendar nine months out, in case one of his kids gets pregnant. He is already planning to make himself available to his unborn grandkids. I think Bob has dove head first into the beauty of selfless living.

Bob is a guy who has the uncomfortable kind of joy. I heard him on a podcast recently, and it was apparent the host was a bit shaken and challenged. The host had the Beatrice-type frustration we talked about earlier. When you feel perplexed and motivated at the same time. But the cool thing is, when we meet someone like Beatrice or Bob, we don't have to leave feeling exasperated. We don't have to believe the lie that their joy is somehow unattainable. We *can* walk in the same kind of joy, because we all have the capability of giving. Whether it is our time, our talents, or our treasure, we all have something to give. This means we can all experience this "giving" kind of joy. But maybe we are afraid to give because our past is super shady. Or we blew it last week and believed we can't help anyone in need because of our mistakes. Let the truth be told. We are just beggars telling other beggars where the food is at. We all blow it. So, let's give. No matter what our past says. People are hungry and need us. Like Snoop Dogg rapped on his recent gospel album, *Bible of Love,* "I'm just a nobody trying to tell everybody, about somebody who can save anybody ..." Let's give. There is some magical joy at the end of this giving rainbow.

I'm pretty sure selfless living and joy are best buds. Two peas in a pod. I think Beatrice, Bob, and Krissy would concur.

THE DUBS

Growing up as a Golden State Warriors' fan wasn't always enjoyable. The "Dubs" lost season after season. We had a few glory days with Chris Mullin, Tim Hardaway, and Mitch

Richmond, but the wins were always short-lived. Watching the Warriors was at times like watching a junior high boys' basketball tournament. Missed layups, grumpy players, and poor draft picks were the norm for The Dubs.

But everything shifted when the Warriors drafted a young point guard from Davidson College named Stephen Curry. And then Klay Thompson. And things continued gaining momentum with new management, a new coach, and a fresh vision. The owners hired coach Steve Kerr and general manager Bob Myers who had keen insight into caring for others. They somehow understood it was the secret sauce to winning. People tend to work harder and play smarter when they know they are valued and loved. If you have watched NBA basketball within the past five years, you know what I'm saying here.

This fresh vision included new core values fueled by unselfishness and a 'giving' attitude. Their tagline became "strength in numbers." It was no longer a solo mission. The team's core values became *"joy, mindfulness, compassion, and competition."* Stop the press! Professional athletes playing basketball with "joy?" Joy was even the first core value mentioned by Steve Kerr in a recent *Sports Illustrated* interview. I couldn't be happier. My favorite team focused on my favorite subject. This unselfish style of basketball has changed the game, with the Warriors leading the league in team assists for four years straight. The Warriors have found both greater joy *and* winning percentages through giving, sharing, and caring.

Let's start sharing the basketball. Others always benefit when we do.

Nevertheless, this joyful play of basketball is only possible with mindfulness and compassion. Competition is a given in any sport but isn't it interesting how it became the last value on the Warrior's list? Mindfulness and compassion require effort. Such principles require a sense of selflessness and a spirit of giving. The simple consideration of others goes a long way. As each player begins to "buy-in" as they share the basketball, let go of 'hero-ball,' and play for one another, joy on the court prevails. By realizing "it's not just about me," the team gets to celebrate a few NBA championships, break some records, and make die-hard Warrior fans extremely happy. Unselfish basketball is fun to watch and leads to championships. Unselfish living is a fun way to exist, and it paves the trail of joy.

AWESOMENESS

Sometimes people just need to hear that they are awesome. Encouraging people with words is a form of serving we sometimes forget to do. Like my four-year-old boy Josiah. Almost daily he looks up at me with those big brown eyes and says, "Dad, you are awesome!" I melt. Or when Michelle and I are having a heated disagreement, he will promptly interrupt us to say, "Mommy, you are pretty. Daddy, you are awesome." It disarms us every time. Such power in words to bring hope and perspective. To shed some joy on our situations.

So, I must ask, when was the last time we looked up from our phone and stopped to ask someone, "Has anyone told you that you are awesome yet today?" People shouldn't have to wait until 8 p.m. to hear they are awesome. If you want to see a physical countenance shift, try it. Simply tell someone they are awesome. It is a practical way to step outside of ourselves for a second. A friendly gesture can do wonders, and it can make someone's day.

They are loved. Guaranteed. I say we let them know.

There are plenty of people out there who need to hear it. How about the employee in the checkout line at your local Trader Joe's? Or the bank teller? Or the lady at the donut shop? Or the janitor in the hallways at school? Or our children? I recently met with a friend who was 26-years-old at the time, and still had never heard his dad say, "I love you." The hardest part about this is his dad was a pastor. He knew his dad loved him, but he just never heard those three precious words.

Let's use words to give life. As we do, joy has a way of sneaking into our countenance. Let's share those words of praise and affirmation. Let's pass out awesomeness. People need that smile of yours. People need your encouragement.

By the way, *you* are awesome! It's true. Jesus just told me.

CHILI PEPPERS

We are meant to share our time on this earth. I think we will discover some joy when we give it away. Let's realize this life is not just about us. Nuns have this truth down pat. I think the Golden State Warriors are on to something. Bob Goff nailed it. My sister lives it. Just like my friend Brad recently said, "When I give more to God, I have more to give." When we give our time, talents and treasures to others, we are ultimately giving to God. Check out the story of the sheep and the goats in Matthew 25:31-46. When we serve people, we are serving Jesus.

I think the Red Hot Chili Peppers have a song about giving things away. Maybe you can hear it now…

Let's roll with it.

Let's chew on the chilies.

Let's share the love.

Let's bring hope to the hopeless.
Joy is waiting.

GIVE

Holding tight, thinking what might –
Be if I decide to share, I'll stop. To stare
Upon those in need rather than fulfill their dreams,
Or mend what seems – to be sad songs of memories
Torn into the fabric of loss – remove the dross which
Hides the silver strand of promised land to
The child of God who –
Looks upon me with eyes wide, yet ... I still pass by.
Staring into the meaningless ocean of media,
Caring more about a "like" or "follow"
Then this person's poverty-stricken tomorrow,
As they then fade – into a position of begging,
All while I continue contemplating –
My position of popularity
And how many people just re-tweeted me.
Think about Maria in India for a moment.
This leper, both blind and lame, festering wounds inflicting pain,
Day after day the same – the –

Same emotions, same discomforts, same longing – for some
comfort
From helping hands or fearless love, to touch the sorrows –
Of loneliness, brokenness, motionless –
For she cannot walk in green meadows or peaceful streams ~
Tears she brings to His table, yet He feeds –
Her soul with hope-filled promise when she just can't take this ...
Sitting on her steps waiting – to sit quietly with her King ...
He then brings
Hope to employ her heart with touch from strangers
Yet tears still linger ...
But giving souls feed her bread, now she says,
I know He loves me, I know He holds me.
I know He feeds me – with
Delicate hands, His bride stands
By me endlessly
Until eternity envelops my song that sings ~
Thankful melodies from the heart that brings
Love & joy through giving ...

PART 3
AT OUR FINGERTIPS

Each day holds a surprise. But only if we expect it can we see, hear, or feel it when it comes to us. Let's not be afraid to receive each day's surprise, whether it comes to us as sorrow or as joy. It will open a new place in our hearts, a place where we can welcome new friends and celebrate more fully our shared humanity.

— Henri Nouwen

CHAPTER 13

CAN I HAVE SOME WATER?

Returning to our "source" of joy – again and again

My wife, Michelle, loves water more than anyone I know. If she could have a weightless and invisible Camelback® attached to her, she would. She even told me the other night, "Remember how wonderful it was when I got to have a catheter at the hospital? I could drink all the water I wanted and never had to get up to pee!" As you can imagine, water is a big deal in our household. Whenever one of the kiddos is lacking energy, has bad breath, or doesn't feel good, the answer is always the same. Drink some water, and it will help. Or as my Navy Division Commander in boot camp might say, "Drink some water and suck it up."

We need water for just about everything—drinking, cooking, cleaning, bathing, swimming, and more. Frequently, when I climb into the rack at night, ready to call upon Dr. Pillow, I'll feel a tap on my shoulder and a gentle whisper, "Honey, can you run downstairs and get me a bottle of water?" Or as I'm drifting off to sleep, one of our boys will shout from the top of his lungs, "Daaaaaaaad!!! Can I have some water?" As much as I honestly want to hammer back, "Go get it yourself you little scoundrel!" or "You go downstairs and grab your little plastic idol filled with tasteless liquid!" I just can't do such a thing. I quickly become a knight in shining armor to quench the thirst of my wife and boys.

Being thirsty is something we are all very familiar with. But for most of us, it's a simple problem to resolve. Our affluent Western society can run the tap, grab a water bottle, or fill a glass from the refrigerator spout. However, many countries, cities, and villages throughout the world can't readily access water. I briefly experienced this struggle during my seasons of life in remote villages in India and small towns in Africa. Whenever we needed water, we had to drop the bucket deep into the well and pull it back up. We continually had to return to the source. The water was available, but it took some initiative to get it. Whether it's simple to retrieve or takes more effort, the point is the same. There is a source of water, and we need to return to the source to get it again and again.

The same is true with joy. It is available, but it takes a little energy to get it. Experiencing joy begins with a few initial steps. Acknowledge our *desire* for it. Take *action* to get it. And finally, be open enough to *receive* it.

DESIRE

Sticking with the water analogy, sometimes we are dehydrated and don't realize it. Frequent headaches, body aches, migraines, weight gain, or fatigue might be plaguing us. Often, all we need to do is increase our H2O intake. To feel better inside and out, we must recognize our raw desire, which is to quench our thirst with some water.

There seems to be a similar battle for joy ... We feel like crap. Our relationships are messy. Real, heartfelt communication is at the bottom of the barrel. Our coworkers are beginning to shy away from us. We go to bed grumpy, only to wake up moody. We want to be lighthearted, joyful and content. Instead, we try to find joy with the funky stuff. The late-night social media binge, taking us down rabbit trails of envy, lust, or worry. The secret popping of a pain pill to numb emotions and seek a new high. The refrigerator raid of bacon, Ho Hos®, and half-n-half. But our thirst still isn't quenched. We are frumpier, angrier, and more irritable.

We are all prone to vices we think will satisfy our craving for happiness. Honestly, I think what we want is lasting joy. It's one of life's greatest desires.

Some recognize this desire early in life, like the legendary John Lennon:

> When I was five years old, my mother always told me that happiness was the key to life. When I went to school, they asked me what I wanted to be when I grew up. I wrote down 'happy.' They told me I didn't understand the assignment, and I told them they didn't understand life.

Others recognize their yearning for happiness mid-way through life, like successful recording artist and record producer Sean "Puffy" Combs:

> I just want to be happy. You know what I'm saying? I just want to be happy, and I want to be able to make somebody else happy.

Then there are those who don't recognize their longing for joy until their final days, like the Dalai Lama who summarizes the entirety of life by stating:

The purpose of our lives is to be happy.

The craving to be happy and experience a life of joy is real. Whether we are five-years-old or 85-years-old, this desire dwells within each of us. It's healthy to want happiness in life. God put such longings for joy in us. But we can't expect another bag of Doritos to bring bliss. Or think other temporary jolts of happiness—money, fame, music, or religion will satisfy us. Yes, these things can be good for some time. But they will never be enough. When it comes to the deep longings of life, *lasting* happiness and joy is only found in the God who created it.

ACTION

If we have recognized our natural desire for joy, then what? We need to take a trip to His well, drop the bucket and fill up. The Psalmist hints at this when he says, "In Your presence *is* fullness of joy." In other words, if we want to find the joy and happiness of God, we need to run into His presence. Just like when we are thirsty, we must go to the source (a grocery store, kitchen sink, or an African well) to get water.

"Well," we may ask, "how can I be in His presence?" "How can I experience His available joy?" First, simply become *aware* of His omnipresence. This means He is all over the place, always. Think about this for a second … I can talk to Him, spend time with Him, and enjoy Him everywhere I go. In my car, in my room, at the gym, at a party, at church, by the fireplace, at the beach, in the forest, under a waterfall, on a hike, while mowing the lawn, washing dishes, or pounding the keyboard at work.

Another practical way to enjoy His presence is to *read* the Scriptures in a solitary location. You might feel His presence on your front porch in the morning with a cup of coffee or while flying on an airplane across the Atlantic Ocean. The cool thing is you can read Scriptures anywhere. The Bible has been the best-selling book in the world for centuries, with an estimated 5 billion copies sold from 1815 – 1975. And now with countless Bible reading apps available, we don't even need a Bible to access God's Word.

You can also encounter the joy of God's presence by taking some time to *worship* Jesus. After all, He did so much for us. Maybe this is the least we can do. Worship is a matter of the heart and expression of our love, so it can come in all shapes, sizes, and measures. And it's not limited to just singing songs on Sunday morning. We can worship God through things like artistic design, dance, construction, cooking, and even through sport. Like Eric Liddell, the Olympic track and field medalist from Great Britain, who expressed his worship of God through running. As he said in the acclaimed *Chariots of Fire,* "I believe God made me for a purpose, but He also made me fast. And when I run, I feel His pleasure." Friends, the pleasure of God can be upon you and I as well! The joy of God can overflow from our lives when we live under His canopy of grace. Let's take some time to worship Him through our passions and gifts. Eric Geiger summarizes this truth well in one of his blog posts, "In Psalm 16, David writes about the joy he has in God. David says, 'He sets the Lord always before Him.' Even in the regular and the mundane, we may sense His pleasure if we 'set the Lord always before us.'" This means, we can feel His pleasure and joy when we _____. Fill in the blank.

Whatever it might be, let's *take action* to experience the wonder of joy in His presence. Let's reach out and accept the invitation to His life of joy today. Listen to His wild offer from the book of Isaiah:

Is anyone thirsty? Come and drink — even if you have
no money!
Come, take your choice of wine or milk — it's all free!
Why spend your money on food that does not give you
strength?
Why pay for food that does you no good?
Listen to me, and you will eat what is good.
You will enjoy the finest food.
Come to me with your ears wide open.
Listen, and you will find life.

RECEIVE

If I go through the hassle of getting out of bed in the middle of the night to fetch my boys some water, it would be awkward and even frustrating if they did not at least take a sip. Or if I ran downstairs to fill Michelle's H2O addiction, and she never took a guzzle, I would be perplexed. The same is true with joy. God went through all kinds of trouble to make joy available for His kids. He walked among us, suffered for us, and eventually died for us. All so we could enter a relationship with Him, be loved by Him, and experience joy with Him. He offers this joy to us in abundance—endless supply, mug overflowing type stuff. We can have as much of Him as we want.

Sometimes, though, my cup gets dry. Other times I don't even pick it up off the shelf. It's getting dusty. Maybe it's time to bust it out again and place it under the fountain. Or dip it deep into the well. When I do, it tends to make a difference in all other areas of my life. My desires are purified, my contentment is deeper, and my relationships get a little bit sweeter. This joy is available, just ask Him. To quote Eugene Peterson's take on Isaiah 12:3-4:

> *Joyfully you'll pull up buckets of water from the wells*
> *of salvation.*
> *And as you do it, you'll say, "Give thanks to God.*
> *Call out His name. Ask Him anything!*
> *Shout to the nations, tell them what He's done,*
> *Spread the news of His great reputation!"*

I suggest we return to the source of joy again and again and again … Let's drink up! It's free.

THIRST

I thirst ...
Quiet longings, thirst for belonging –
Begin with responding to the reality of who He is ...
Well of living water.
Cup filled with a joyful stream, no longer a dream ~
now aware of His proximity.
Elation accessible, no longer a fable, present at the table –
of mercy, grace, and song.
Pages opened to unfolding opportunity of delightful beauty,
free from cruelty once bound by pain.
I thirst ...
For the water of truth to wash over this dry heart ~
quench the undeniable yearning with hope.
Touch my arid mouth with –
everlasting, never-fading, always remaining
joy ...
I heard You say this once – I thirst ...
For pure affection from your bride,
jubilation of reunion between lovers.
For dove's eyes to be met with eternal fixation – this contemplation ~
how You would transform the sinful manipulation I once believed
to become the devoted participation in loving and intimate streams.
I thirst ...
Taste the water, it's free. Come to the well, it's deep.
Sip from the cup, it's meek ...
Thirst leads to source ~
of joy, of life,
drink of the purity, savor the mercy –
leave the strife, the sorrow, the fears of unknown tomorrows.
I thirst. I drink. I'm free.

CHAPTER 14

BELLS, BABIES & BREAD

The joyful celebration of new life ...

WEDDING BELLS

She was stunning! Dressed in white, eyes sparkling, smile beaming, and skin glowing. The months, weeks, days, and hours of preparation finally led us to this day. As she set her eyes on mine and made her way down the aisle, I could hardly breathe. The anticipated joy was now filling our lives. Michelle and I entered holy matrimony on May 8, 2004, and it will forever be one of the most joy-filled days of my life! The wedding ceremony squeezed out tears of happiness, with family and friends embracing our love for one another. We even had a sweet make-out session in front of 250 of our friends and family. Our reception was icing on the cake. We enjoyed a scrumdiddlyumptious tri-tip dinner, the finest hors-d'oeuvres and a dance party like it was 1999 with DJ Bunny laying down funk tracks on the turntables. We danced the night away, laughed with the twinkling stars above us and entered the wild adventure of marriage. JOY is the one-word, which floods my soul when I think of our wedding day. Cup to the brim, bubbling over, flowing like the Amazon River kind of joy. We entered a covenant with one another, promised not to give up and stepped foot on a pathway for deep and vulnerable human love.

Similarly, joy fills the dance floors of heaven when a man makes a covenant with God through Jesus Christ. When we express faith in Jesus, heaven throws a Jammy-Jam! It's true. Jesus said so. Jesus shared a story about this kind of excitement:

Or what woman, having ten silver coins, if she loses one coin, does not light a lamp, sweep the house, and search carefully until she finds it? And when she has found it, she calls her friends and neighbors together, saying, 'Rejoice with me, for I have found the piece which I lost!' Likewise, I say to you, there is joy in the presence of the angels of God over one sinner who repents.

All heaven celebrates when one feeble sinner repents and responds through faith in Jesus. God hosts the after-party when one of His children is set free from the bondage of sin and death.

BABIES CHANGE THINGS

The birth of my firstborn son, Isaac, was quite the experience. It all started with "the call" from my wife to go to the hospital, as her water had just broken, and our baby was getting ready to pop out. So, as every reasonable and excited new father should do, I swung by Jiffy Lube for an oil change. I wanted to make sure the car ran well on the way to the hospital. After exchanging pleasantries with the Jiffy Lube guy and deciding whether to get a new air filter, I felt like I was ready to become a dad. I then rushed home, came bounding through the door, loaded my pregnant, laboring wife into the lubed car and entered the realms of parenting like a state champion.

Ten hours later, Michelle was deep into the pains of labor, screaming loud enough to make an ant wiggle and sending nurses into pandemonium. During a brief pause in labor, I decided to walk down to the parking lot and grab a few things from the car. But upon my return, I was surprised to see the doctors prepping my wife for an epidural. I guess everyone was ready for her to calm down a bit.

Before I knew it, I was being asked to hold her still as they stabbed a fat, 18-gauge needle in her spine. Boy was this was a game changer! Once we threw the "natural birth" idea out the window, we went from pains up the yin-yang to a yoga serenity soundtrack and me watching Monday Night Football. The doctors and nurses monitored her progress as I took cat naps in a squishy lounge chair as any supportive husband should. About four hours later, Isaac was ready to come out. This was when the fun began, and life would never be the same.

Once he exited the birth canal, I cut the cord and thought we would be off to the races. But there was a hang-up. He happened to inhale some meconium junk on the way out, which caused breathing issues. Inhaling meconium is like sucking a sticky mud puddle into your lungs and then trying to breathe. Our son was rushed up to the Neonatal Intensive Care Unit to spend the first week of his life with IVs, antibiotics, breathing treatments, and a lot of nurses. It was a rough start for our little buddy. We got to know the staff a bit, eat hospital food and work the night shift with Isaac. But the meds soon worked, and within a week we got to carry him through our front door. When the door shut behind us, we entered the wild world of diapers, sleepless nights, and frequent baby barf on our shoulders. True, abundant joy from this new life now filled our home. Eleven years later, he still barfs on our shoulder occasionally and sometimes causes a few sleepless nights. But he brings us genuine laughter and intrigues us with attorney-level intelligence every day.

I share this story because it ties into our redemption and joy with Jesus. Due to the weight of sin, we entered this world with some major troubles, pains, and spiritual sickness. Yet Jesus, the Great Physician, intercedes on our behalf and breathes life into our lungs—a life that will carry us into His Father's eternal home one day.

Have we welcomed His gentle and intensive care? Are we allowing Him to turn our pains into promises, our sadness into strength, or our sorrows into joy?

A BIG DEEP BREATH

Finding a lost child is a super big deal. A couple of months ago my neighbor's five-year-old son went missing. Our entire cul-de-sac will never forget the sound of his frightened mother screaming from the top of her lungs, "Jack! Where are you, Jack?" We all went searching. I hopped on my bike and drove around the neighborhood looking for little Jack. Hearts were beating fast, and other neighbors began to pop their heads out of their doors. All of us parents were on a frantic hunt to find this boy. Even the neighborhood kids were desperately looking for Jack. Time was short because it was just after sunset and the night was rolling in. Fear swept through the neighborhood as shouts of his name rippled up and down the streets.

Fortunately, this frantic and fearful moment only lasted about 15 minutes. By God's grace, we found little Jack being walked back to his house by a local family who noticed a lost and fearful child. Jack's mom ran to her little boy, scooped him up in her arms and held him tight. I'm so thankful this story ended well because millions have not. My heart breaks every time I see the pictures of missing children. But in this case, Jack was found safe. We all took a big breath and exhaled our fears. Us parents hugged our kids a bit tighter that night.

Experiencing this moment of anxiety helped me see the desperation of God's heart in a whole new way. When we are lost, or separated from our Heavenly Father, all heaven joins together to call out our name. Angels are calling our name. God's kids are trying to help bring us to back home. God is calling out as He did in the Garden of Eden, "Adam, *where are you?*"

When we see ourselves as sons and daughters, we see why Jesus went to such great lengths to find us. We can know why the Holy Spirit will go through fire to reach us. We see the desperation of His heart to rescue us, find us and redeem us.

When God captures the heart of a lost soul, it is as if heaven takes a big deep breath. Finally! The wait and search are over. Just as crazy joy-filled my life was on our wedding day, or during the reunion of little Jack and his mommy–the joy of God fills heaven when The Light of the World lights up the dark caves of a repentant sinner's heart.

ANGEL FOOD CAKE

Michelle and I look at each other in bewilderment as we make yet another trip to the grocery store. The insatiable appetites of our three young boys frequently empty our cupboards and refrigerator. It's nutzo! But our devotion to them outweighs our perplexed minds every time. When they ask for bread – we won't dare give them a stone in return. Why? Because we love our kids. We desire to meet the real cravings of their precious little bodies.

I recently came across a similar story in the Old Testament. The nation of Israel had just escaped the grips of an evil tyrant in Egypt. For over 400 years, they were under his heavy hand, bound in the confines of slavery and grueling labor. Yet the faithfulness of a Heavenly Father prevailed, and His love broke through. He called out a humble man (Moses), utilized his willing heart, and with 10 exhaustive plagues, he helped deliver God's people from the world's most powerful man.

I'm sure the people had different expectations of what life would be like after crossing the Red Sea. Dreams of greatness and relaxation, ideas of sipping sweet tea by the riverside and hopes of long Saturday afternoon naps in the hammock. But if you know the story, quite the opposite happened. After the triumphant exit and newfound blessing of freedom, they soon were caught in dusty windstorms amidst a desert wasteland for the next 40 years. It would be as if we had been on a camping trip in the Mohave Desert of California since 1978. I love camping and all, but man … that's a long time.

Naturally, this group of 1 million+ had some hunger pains and missed the tasty tidbits they once had in Egypt. Numbers 11:5 describes a bit of their longing, "We remember the fish we used to eat for free in Egypt. And we had all the cucumbers, melons, leeks, onions, and garlic we wanted." Before you criticize them, imagine what food would be like without garlic and onions for over 40 years. A serious trial.

And even though their complaints grieved the Lord, He stayed true to His character as a compassionate Father who meets the needs of His kids. How, you might ask? Manna.

What is "manna?" The people of Israel asked the same question, as *manna* literally means "What is that?" And in even greater depth of research, Easton notes, "The name is commonly taken as derived from *man*, an expression of surprise, 'What is it?' but more probably it is derived from *manan*, meaning 'to allot,' and hence denoting an 'allotment' or a "gift." Manna was both a mystery and a great gift given to His people in need. God provided angel food cake daily for close to 14,400 days. True story once again. The Psalmist records His faithfulness to Israel by stating, "But he commanded the skies to open; he opened the doors of heaven. He rained down manna for them to eat; he gave them bread from heaven. They ate the food of angels! God gave them all they could hold." Amazing!

I think we receive joy in the same way. Joy is an incredible mystery *and* a wonderful gift from God. The people of Israel longed for food. And each morning there it was, waiting for them. Just like the discontented Israelites, there is an undeniable longing for something more, ringing through the halls of every human heart. People are disgruntled with life, looking to the past for answers, hoping for something better in the future. While all along, God himself is expectantly waiting to feed us the food of angels. This angel food is the joy of God. And there is one word that opens the oven – JESUS.

Without Jesus, this idea of joy disappears faster than a jackrabbit running from a grizzly bear. There is no lasting joy without Jesus in the picture. When Jesus is welcome in the room, joy adorns every corner. Jesus lights up the place like fireworks on Independence Day. As C.S. Lewis said, "He himself is the fuel our spirits were designed to burn or the food our spirits were designed to feed on. There is no other."

Think about when Jesus was a wedding guest. He did far more than sing some karaoke songs or dance the running man on center stage. He brought His smile to the party. When His mom asked him for a favor, He responded with a twinkle in His eye and turned plain ole' water into the finest of wine. Knowing this, rocks my worldview. Because it means Jesus really isn't the Swedish, blonde-haired, serious guy wearing a halo holding up two fingers like a guru. He is the life of the party and drew people in with His genuine soul. Jesus is the kind of guy who sits by the lonely junior high kid in the corner at the school dance. He is also the guy willing to give the best man speech at a wedding. Jesus was incredibly mindful of others. His years on earth were observant, sincere, and full of high levels of emotional intelligence. His gentle nature brought joy to a room and joy in every moment.

If you are like me, sometimes when we see a big block of Scripture in a book, we may skip over it thinking, "I've heard this before." But this passage of Scripture is vital to understand Jesus' love for people and His attention to joy. Take a look:

The next day there was a wedding celebration in the village of Cana in Galilee. Jesus' mother was there, and Jesus and his disciples were also invited to the celebration. The wine supply ran out during the festivities, so Jesus' mother told him, "They have no more wine." "Dear woman, that's not our problem," Jesus replied. "My time has not yet come." But his mother told the servants, "Do whatever he tells you." Standing nearby were six stone water jars, used for Jewish ceremonial washing. Each could hold twenty to thirty gallons. Jesus told the servants, "Fill the jars with water." When the jars had been filled, He said, "Now dip some out, and take it to the master of ceremonies." So, the servants followed His instructions. When the master of ceremonies tasted the water that was now wine, not knowing where it had come from (though, of course, the servants knew), he called the bridegroom over. "A host always serves the best wine first," he said. "Then, when everyone has had a lot to drink, he brings out the less expensive wine. But you have kept the best until now!" This miraculous sign at Cana in Galilee was the first time Jesus revealed His glory. And his disciples believed in him.

Going above and beyond is typical Jesus style. The wedding was full of joy because Jesus was present and welcome. Jesus' disciples saw His joyful glory and believed. Even the water responded to His presence. As Alexander Pope describes this miracle by stating, "The conscious water saw its Master and blushed."

Joy is simply a response to the reality of Jesus.

I realize joy can be a mystery like the manna in the wilderness at times. But the truth is – we need it. And God has plenty of it. Ask Him for some, and you get a whole lot of Jesus. Let's eat this heavenly food. He wants us to. As He said to the nation of Israel, "For it was I, the Lord your God, who rescued you from the land of Egypt. Open your mouth wide, and I will fill it with good things."

He has a table of joy set for you and me, His beloved. I think it's time to attend His feast.

ILLUMINATE
Ideas in color.
Brilliant lights, vibrant and bright,
stimulating sight ~ transforming the night
into a story of joy for senses
to embrace a fascination with grace – allowing eyes to see.
Ideas in color.
Flowers in bloom, turning the room,
Into a place of rest for the weary and broken.
Placed in hand, planted in land, softening heart of man
to win the one He loves.
Ideas in color.
Painting canvas upon streams of blue, mountains of white,
green meadows hue ~ emotions delight
in the artistry of the One who thought of ...
sunshine picnics and eating with chopsticks,
climbing trees and bumble bees, roses and leaves,
streaming His design of joyful majesty.

CHAPTER 15

HONEYMOON BABIES

Intimacy produces spiritual kids

I've been asked a few times to name my favorite book of the Bible. I have my "Top 10" list, but so often I'm drawn back to this small book of poetry in the Old Testament called The Song of Songs (aka The Song of Solomon). Now if you have ever read this book, you soon realize it is a pretty intense honeymoon-type poem. And its old-school lyrics can make a reader blush, for its intimate language describes the mutual affection between husband and wife. I remember reading The Song of Songs in its entirety the morning before my wedding. I was gearing up for every man's favorite part of getting married: the honeymoon.

Mainly because really, really, really good things happen on the honeymoon.

But sometimes, things come out of honeymoons. Life-changing things like … babies. When a couple gets intimate, God created the supernaturally natural ability for a woman to become pregnant. Quite a few of our friends conceived their first child on their honeymoon. And the rest is history. Honeymoon babies are real. It's because intimate moments between husband

and wife poses the potential of producing kids. It's remarkable how something, which gives so much pleasure also results in a living and breathing human being.

Why am I talking about all this mushy stuff, if this is supposed to be a book about "joy?" It's because I think joy is a child of intimacy. If we lack intimacy with Jesus, our joy is short-lived and fades away when life sucks.

Intimacy with God = Joy. And Joy = Strength.

Everything flows out of intimacy.

I remember writing Pastor Britt Merrick an email just before moving to Argentina. I was asking for advice on church planting, ministry, and the like. He was kind enough to answer, and his short reply still challenges me to this day. "The best strategy in ministry is to practice continual intimacy with Christ! Make Him your supreme joy and learn to enjoy Him at all times and you will never lack for unction."

It is worth saying again. Everything flows out of intimacy.

This intimacy is why I like the Song of Songs so much. It's not just the cool phrases I get to tell my wife. Like how her hair is like a flock of goats or her teeth remind me of shorn sheep. But because these descriptive terms in God's Word *also* point to the level of spiritual intimacy Jesus desires from his Bride, the Church. Please hear me out. I'm not making a theological or hermeneutical discussion out of this. I'm not going toe to toe with Bible scholars on this one. I'm just saying, if I put on my spiritual lens with a dose of maturity, I can embrace this book of the Bible with affection and purpose. I think there is a significant reason for why the massively impactful 19th Century preacher Charles Spurgeon considered this his favorite book of the Bible. Or why the influential ministry leader named Mike Bickle, who leads the International House of Prayer, was said to have done a 12-year study on the Song of Songs. That is a serious deep dive. But look at the unction and fruit born from such intimacy. The International House of Prayer he helped start in Kansas City, has had a running prayer meeting 24/7 since September 19, 1999. Dang!

Yes, I am called to adore my wife as described in this book of Scripture, and she should occasionally tell me my eyes are like doves by the rivers of waters and washed with milk. But when was the last time we looked at Jesus in this way? As my Heavenly Bridegroom? Are we taking time to look upon Him with eyes of affection? When was the last time we stopped to hear Him sing a song over us, gently inviting us to come away with Him, so that He can hear our voice (Song of Solomon 2:13-14)?

Jesus loves us, His Bride, whom He laid his life down for. And He invites us to a deeper place of intimacy with Him. The truth is, I can go as deep with God as I'd like to. The door to His heart is wide open. How deep will we go?

FOUR LEVELS OF SPIRITUAL INTIMACY

FIRST LEVEL

When we begin a relationship with God, we surrender to Him as *Lord*. We talked about this idea of surrender a couple of chapters back. We get our feet wet when we recognize **Him as Master and as the Good Shepherd.**

SECOND LEVEL

Then, if we are brave enough, we go even deeper and refer to **God as Abba *Father*, aka Daddy.** Earlier in the book, we talked about how He really is a good Father who adores and cares for His children more than we can imagine.

THIRD LEVEL

The next level of depth is what I call *friendship* **with God**. Toward the end of His earthly ministry, Jesus began to refer to His disciples as His friends. They had spent quality time together, shared meals together, and traveled together for years. Then you have Old Testament examples like Abraham, who was known as a "friend of God." Friendship with God is merely a more profound form of intimacy. For example, I now acknowledge my dad as one of my closest friends. But it wasn't always that way. He was first my earthly father, but with time, trust, and depth of relationship, we have become really good friends over the years. Our relationship took on a new form of intimacy. I think the same is true with God. When we are willing to go deeper with Him, we enter the world of friendship with the Friend who sticks closer than a brother.

FOURTH LEVEL

Now the final stage of intimacy is a bit more challenging, especially for us guys. It's the intimate invitation to **know Jesus as** *Lover*. This is the sacred ground, the circle of trust-type stuff. It's the take off your shoes, burning bush, face-to-face, feet washing with tears kind of thing. It's the intimate places of our hearts and lives. The room where nobody else is welcome. Like the marriage bed a husband and wife share where no others are welcome. I believe there is a sacred place reserved in our hearts where only Jesus can go. The holy place of intimacy, which transcends words. A place where we invite Him into our deepest fears, longings, hopes, unspoken dreams and greatest affections. It's where we allow the nail-scarred hands of Christ to touch the most sacred and private aspects of our lives. This is the place He longs to bring us. The place where we hold nothing back and He has *all* of us. "I am my Lover's, and my Lover is mine" (Song of Solomon 6:3).

It is in this sacred and intimate place we can sing:

I am Yours, You are mine
I'm Your cup, pour out Your wine
I'm Your candle Lord, You make me shine
I am Yours, You are mine.

Everything flows out of intimacy.

Joy is the beloved child and spiritual fruit of intimacy with Jesus. There is just no way around it.

INTIMATE IDENTITY

This clever Creator crafted each of us—giving us each a distinct narrative. We all have a story. Just look at your fingers. Those tips of your fingers are pretty hip. Amazing actually. And the God of the Universe is *intimately* acquainted with each line, groove, and curve. Just listen to what my friend Jeff told me about fingerprints. Fingerprints are part of his job after all, as he is a product manager of engineering at an identity solutions provider. These cold hard facts give us all a better idea of this phenomenon and how it relates to our story.

- Fingerprints begin developing in the tenth week of the pregnancy – several weeks before gender is apparent. And at 17 weeks of pregnancy, a baby's fingerprints have been established.
- According to some, it's the pressure between the top and third layer of skin, which causes the ridges to form in the middle (*basal*) layer; thus, creating a unique fingerprint.
- Other variables believed to impact fingerprints include hormone levels, oxygen levels in the blood, blood pressure, pressure with which the fetus touches

surroundings within the womb. Because of these variables, the chance of identical fingerprints has never happened. The culmination of these factors brings variation to each fingerprint from finger-to-finger, hand-to-hand. Even identical twins do not share fingerprints.

The detail is amazing, and it supports the truth that we each have a unique story and identity. So how does this relate to joy? It's because God desires for *His joy* to mark those fingerprints of yours. He longs to weave *His joy* throughout the intricate pages of your book. But this can only happen if we let Him into the idiosyncratic moments of our personal lives.

I suggest an unembellished increase of Jesus in our life.

Let Him ride shotgun on our drive to work. Have Him accompany our afternoon jog as our running buddy. Chat with Him as we pour our morning coffee. Recognize His presence with us while watching a movie. Welcome Him into the details of the daily bustle. Invite Him into the quiet moments of pain or the embarrassing moments of shame. Celebrate with Him in moments of triumph. Live a life so intimately acquainted with Jesus, that our fingerprints leave behind His oil of gladness everywhere we go.

After all, sharing His joy in every aspect of our journey can make all the difference. The world wants it. They need it. Let's get to know Jesus a little more each day. For if we know Him, we will make Him known.

****

LANDING THE PLANE

We have flown with this idea of joy for quite a few pages now. I think it's a good time to land the airplane. So, as we prepare for landing, I believe the Captain of our souls wants to remind us of a couple of things.

Let us remember to look up occasionally and witness Him. The God of joy at work in our midst. Be it in His creation or in His character, when we look for joy in Him, we find it.

Let's allow His joy to mark each page of our never-ending story. Let's move past the writer's block and allow the Author of our narrative to put His pen to work. Uproot the foul roots that are killing us. Plant some healthy roots to sustain us in the difficult times. Stick some dynamite in those dams blocking the river of joy He has promised us. And when we feel locked out of the bounce house of joy, reach deep in those pockets and pull out the keys of love and obedience. His love has a gentle way of reminding us how saying yes to Him is pretty fun. Let's open the door to joy and jump around. Let's laugh a little, look for beauty in the ashes, and step outside of ourselves to serve someone in need. Joy awaits.

Finally, let us notice how close the joy we long for really is. We can dip our cup into His well of joy again and again. His mercy is new and fresh every morning and His abundant life is literally at our fingertips.

After all this, I want to ask this question once again, *"Where's the Joy?"*

Oh! There it is! With Jesus.

CLOSER

Sitting next to You. Sky blue, heart true,
quiet love. Through –
Good times. Bad. Happy. Sad.
Reminding me ... I am ~ Your child, Your lad.
Your friend. Then – You pose a suggestion ...
"Keep close, never leave, stand next to Me –
wear My heart on your sleeve, stop to breathe, just believe and see –
The joy of My intimacy."
You welcome me to the deep & forgetful sea –
Of love, of joy, of life, of grace.
Lord, I love You! I love Your face,
Your smile. Carrying close through trial still mile after mile –
The countenance of peace, the love You bring, the song You sing,
I found my belonging. – In the
Strong Savior of Story ~
Weeping night now morning glory, transforming
The narrative from sadness to pouring –
Showers of blessing restoring.
Hallelujah!
Your joy is my strength. Your joy is my life!
I can move forward, toward – the chronicle of joyful meaning,
The singers are singing ~
Joy to the World, the King of Kings has redeemed
Every chapter, every page
Of this joy-filled story.

EPILOGUE

If you have made it this far, I tip my cap and thank you for walking down this path alongside me, as we search for joy together. Life gets pretty exciting when we realize joy can be the oil on the fingerprints we leave behind. Joy really can be the theme of our story. It's pretty cool. I hope you were blessed and continue to pursue the God of joy who fills our lives with adventure, whimsy, and puts a skip in our step! Joy is one of the most contagious and effective character traits we can possess.

Joy changes things. I hope it has changed you as it has me! ☺

ACKNOWLEDGMENTS

JESUS. You are my everything!

Michelle. Your encouragement, patience, and mutual love for adventure puts wind in my sails. Thanks for taking this journey with me! You amaze me. I love you.

Isaac. Your mind is brilliant, your whit is sharp, and your love for story keeps life exciting.

Kai. You have a gift, my son. Let it shine. Bring your message of creativity to the world.

Josiah. Bubby. You bring a smile to every face and make all feel welcome. Keep loving.

Pops. My true mentor. Your journey and example have influenced me beyond words.

Mamma. Your love, your prayers, your listening ear have given me life.

Sis. You are a treasure to this earth. Abundant laughs, altered voices, and kinship.

To the brave souls who let me share your story: *Nick, Dar, & Owen; Brandon & Jennifer; Ole; Phil W.; Jeremy C.* / Thank you for contributing such lasting joy in my life!

To my fantastic editor, *Nicole Edwards.* Your patience and encouragement through this process have been incredible. Thank you! / *Ethan, Russell, Jordan F. & Brent V.* Thanks for your priceless insight and contributions!

Jarrid Wilson. Thanks for helping me get this ball rolling!

Morgan James Publishing. Thank you for taking a chance with me.

ABOUT THE AUTHOR

Danny Williamson is an author, storyteller and itinerant speaker passionate about joy in both domestic and international settings. He holds a bachelor's degree in religion and a master's degree in executive leadership. Danny is currently the executive director for Speaking Louder Ministries *(Jeremy Camp, Founder)*, and the chief joy officer at The Collective Global, a cultural consulting firm. Danny has more than 16 years of leadership and ministry experience, serving as a Hospital Corpsman in the U.S. Navy, a co-founder and director of a non-profit mission organization, a church-planting missionary in Argentina, and an associate pastor in CA.

Originally from San Diego, Danny now resides in Nashville, Tennessee with his wife Michelle and their three adventurous young boys—Isaac, Malakai and Josiah. He enjoys coffee, jet lag, camping, jogging, poetry, date nights with his bride, and wrestling with his boys.

CONNECT WITH DANNY

Danny would love to hear from you and can be emailed directly at **hello@dannywilliamson.com**.

You can also follow him on Instagram **@dannycwilliamson**.

Danny would love to spread some joy with your team, organization, church, conference, or school … If you would like to invite Danny to speak, simply go to:

dannywilliamson.com
whereisthejoybook.com

REFERENCES

INTRODUCTION AND CHAPTER 1: HALF 'N HALF

1. Davis, C. "Joy," in *Evangelical Dictionary of Theology – 2nd Edition*, ed. Walter A. Elwell, (Grand Rapids, MI: Baker Book House Company, 2001).

CHAPTER 2: THE EPIDEMIC OF TEXT NECK

1. Spurgeon, Charles H. *The Treasury of David* (Grand Rapids, MI: Kregel Classics, 1976), 160.

2. Tozer, A.W. *The Pursuit of God* (Abbotsford, WI: Life Sentence Publishing, Inc., 2015), 6.

3. Abdullah, M. Retrieved from https://greatergood.berkeley.edu/article/item/three_tips_for_parents_to_put_away_their_phones

4. Divecha, D. Retrieved from https://greatergood.berkeley.edu/article/item/how_teens_today_are_different_from_past_generations

5. Zacharias, Ravi. "The Pursuit of Meaning: Regaining the Wonder, Part 1." *RZIM: Let My People Think Broadcasts*. Podcast audio, December 2, 2017. Retrieved from https://itunes.apple.com/us/podcast/the-pursuit-of-meaning-regaining-the-wonder-part-1/id1174079089?i=1000395528558&mt=2

6. Psalm 36:8, *New Living Translation.*

CHAPTER 3: YOU DIDN'T HAVE TO DO THAT!

1. Psalm 19:1-4, *New Living Translation.*
2. http://oceanrealmimages.com/blog/23/04/12/ghost-pipefish-facts-and-images.
3. http://www.huffingtonpost.com/2014/07/21/food-quotes-famous-eating_n_2481583.html.
4. https://www.christianquotes.info/search-for-a-quote/#ixzz4q9CNHaun.
5. Zephaniah 3:17, *New Living Translation*
6. Nehemiah 8:10, *New Living Translation*

CHAPTER 4: THAT'S NOT MY NAME

1. Isaiah 52:5a-6, *New Living Translation.*
2. https://jesusculture.com/albums/love-has-a-name/.
3. Isaiah 61:3, *New Living Translation.*
4. Psalm 71:20, *New Living Translation.*
5. http://christian-quotes.ochristian.com/christian-quotes_ochristian.cgi?query=redeem&action=Search&x=0&y=0.
6. Job 42:10, *New Living Translation.*
7. Psalm 130:7-8, *New Living Translation.*
8. Miller, Donald. *Father Fiction.* HOWARD BOOKS, 2010. iBooks. p. 81.
9. Psalm 68:5-6a, *New Living Translation.*
10. Miller, Donald. *Father Fiction.* 2010. iBooks. p. 16.
11. https://thefatherlessgeneration.wordpress.com/statistics/.

CHAPTER 5: ROOTS IS A LONG MINI-SERIES

1. Ryzik, Melena. 2016. The return of 'roots,' in a new era: Seminal 1977 mini-series about slavery is recreated with attention to accuracy. *International New York Times* 2016.

2. "IT'S ALL GOOD: Here's a Challenge for You: Let Go of Hate." *Vaughan Citizen*, Jan 29, 2015. 1, http://ezproxy.liberty.edu/login?url=https://search-proquest-com.ezproxy.liberty.edu/docview/1649051557?accountid=12085.

3. Lucado, M. Retrieved from: http://www.coatscounsel.net/bitterness-part-ii/

4. Hosea 10:12, *New Living Translation.*

5. Hebrews 12:15, *New Living Translation.*

6. Philippians 4:4-7, *Easy-to-Read Version (ERV).* Copyright © 2006 by Bible League International.

7. Retrieved from http://pza.sanbi.org/boscia-albitrunca.

8. Retrieved from http://sunnyfortuna.com/explore/redwoods_and_water.htm.

9. Colossians 2:7, *New Living Translation*, italics mine.

CHAPTER 6: THAT DAM RIVER

1. *USA Today,* Timothy Sexton, Leaf Group; Updated March 21, 2018 http://traveltips.usatoday.com/hoover-dam-4890.html.

2. Lieb, Anna. Retrieved on 13 January, 2018: http://www.pbs.org/wgbh/nova/next/earth/dam-removals/.

3. Brown, Brené. Retrieved on 24 January, 2018: https://www.ted.com/talks/brene_brown_on_vulnerability?utm_campaign=tedspread--a&utm_medium=referral&utm_source=tedcomshare.

4. Brown, Brené. *Braving the Wilderness: The Quest for True Belonging and the Courage to Stand Alone* (New York, NY: Random House, 2017), 144.

CHAPTER 7: HAVE YOU SEEN MY KEYS?

1. Blackaby, H. Retrieved on February 23, 2018 from http://christian-quotes.ochristian.com/christian-quotes_ochristian.cgi?query=loved+by+God&action=Search&x=0&y=0

2. Goff, Bob. *Love Does: Discover a Secretly Incredible Life in an Ordinary World.* Nashville, TN: Thomas Nelson. 2012.

3. Moody, D.L. Retrieved on February 23, 2018 from http://christian-quotes.ochristian.com/christian-quotes_ochristian.cgi?query=obedience&action=Search&x=0&y=0

4. John 15:9-10, italics mine, *English Standard Version.*

CHAPTER 8: LOVE LESSONS FROM MT. KILIMANJARO

1. John 3:16, *New Living Translation.*

2. 1 John 4:8, *New Living Translation.*

3. Lewis, C.S. *The Beloved Works of C.S. Lewis: The Four Loves* (New York, NY: Inspirational Press, A Division of BBS Publishing Corporation, 1960), 281.

4. Nouwen, Henri JM. *In the name of Jesus: Reflections on Christian leadership.* St Paul's BYB, 1999.

CHAPTER 9: FOLLOW THE PROMPTINGS

1. Keller, Timothy J. Retrieved from *azquotes.com.* URL: http://www.azquotes.com/quote/672403.

2. Keller, Timothy J. *The reason for God: Belief in an age of skepticism.* Penguin, 2008.

3. Deuteronomy 30:19, *New Living Translation.*

CHAPTER 10: FIVE-YEAR-OLDS CAN'T DRIVE

1. American Heart Association. "Humor helps your heart? How?" www.heart.org, April 5, 2017. http://www.heart.org/ HEARTORG/HealthyLiving/Humor-helps-your-heart-How_ UCM_447039_Article.jsp#.Wsd0xmaZOu5.

2. Proverbs 17:22, *New Living Translation.*

3. The Journal.ie. "How often do you smile? Adults only manage 20 a day...380 times less than children. Two Dublin teenagers have come up with a project to try and get people to smile more.," www.thejournal.ie, July 2, 2014. accessed April 6, 2018, http://jrnl.ie/1550017.

4. Berg, Hanna. Söderlund, Magnus. Lindström, Annika. "Spreading joy: examining the effects of smiling models on consumer joy and attitudes." Journal of Consumer Marketing 32/6 (2015), 459–469. © Emerald Group Publishing Limited ISSN 0736-3761. DOI 10.1108/JCM-03-2015-1356.

5. Dietrich Bonhoeffer. *Life Together: The Classic Exploration of Christian Community.* (New York, NY: Harper Collins Publishers, 1954). 78.

6. Proverbs 18:1, *Amplified Bible.*

7. Holt-Lunstad, Julianne. Smith, Timothy. Baker, Mark. Harris, Tyler. Stephenson, David. "Loneliness and Social Isolation as Risk Factors for Mortality: A Meta-Analytic Review". Perspectives on Psychological Science 2015, Vol. 10(2) 227 –237. DOI 10.1177/1745691614568352

8. Swindoll, Charles. Retrieved on April 6, 2018 from https:// www.brainyquote.com/quotes/quotes/c/charlesrs121433.html.

9. Brown, Brené. Retrieved on April 6, 2018 from https://www. brainyquote.com/quotes/brene_brown_553096.

CHAPTER 11: AMERICA'S MOST WANTED

1. Matthew 28:20, *New Living Translation.*
2. Feinberg, M. *Fight Back with Joy: Celebrate More. Regret Less. Stare Down Your Greatest Fears.* (Franklin, TN: Worthy Books, 2015), 62.
3. Psalm 16:11, *New King James Version* **(NKJV)**. Copyright © 1982 by Thomas Nelson. Italics mine.
4. Thompson, F. "The Hound of Heaven". Retrieved on April 27, 2018 from http://www.bartleby.com/236/239.html.
5. Smithers, D. *Count Zinzendorf & The Moravians: Prayer Makes History.* Retrieved on April 27, 2018 from http://www.thetravelingteam.org/articles/count-zinzendorf-the-moravians-prayer-makes-history.
6. Hutton, J.E. *History of the Moravian Church* (1909). Retrieved on April 27, 2018 from http://www.ccel.org/ccel/hutton/moravian.v.vi.html.

CHAPTER 12: NUNS & BASKETBALL

1. Ballard, Chris. *No coach, no problem.* Sports Illustrated Magazine, May 29, 2017.
2. Peppers, Red Hot Chili. Kiedis, Anthony. Frusciante, Flea, John. Smith, Chad. "Give It Away". *Blood sugar sex magik.* Warner Bros., 1991.

PART 3 INTRO:

1. Lloyd-Jones, Martin. *Joy Unspeakable: Power and Renewal in the Holy Spirit* (Sussex, England: Kingsway Publications, 1984), 102.

CHAPTER 13: CAN I HAVE SOME WATER?

1. Retrieved from http://www.azquotes.com/quote/416317?ref=i-just-want-to-be-happy, Ibid.
2. Retrieved from https://www.brainyquote.com/quotes/dalai_lama_132971?src=t_happy
3. Psalm 16:11, *New King James Version.*
4. Retrieved from http://www.guinnessworldrecords.com/world-records/best-selling-book-of-non-fiction/.
5. Geiger, E. Retrieved from https://ericgeiger.com/2014/03/i-feel-gods-pleasure-when-i-blank/.
6. Isaiah 55:1-3, *New Living Translation.*
7. Isaiah 12:3-4, The Message **(MSG)** Copyright © 1993, 1994, 1995, 1996, 2000, 2001, 2002 by Eugene H. Peterson.

CHAPTER 14: BELLS, BABIES & BREAD

1. Easton, M. "Manna – Easton's Bible Dictionary." Blue Letter Bible. Last Modified 24 Jun, 1996. https://www.blueletterbible.org//search/Dictionary/viewTopic.cfm
2. Psalm 78:23-25, *New Living Translation.*
3. Lewis, C.S. retrieved from http://christian-quotes.ochristian.com/christian-quotes_ochristian.cgi?query=He+Himself+is&action=Search&x=0&y=0.
4. John 2:1-11, *New Living Translation.*
5. Zacharias, R. *The Mission of an Evangelist.* "Evangelistic Preaching in the 21st Century" (Minneapolis, MN: World Wide Publications, 2001), 59.
6. Hebrews 12:2, *New Living Translation,* italics mine.
7. https://www.blueletterbible.org//search/Dictionary/viewTopic.cfm.
8. Psalm 81:10, *New Living Translation.*

9. The Holy Bible, *New King James Version.* Luke 15:8-10.

CHAPTER 15: HONEYMOON BABIES

1. Retrieved on May 17, 2018 from https://www.ihopkc.org/about/.

2. Kilpatrick, Bob (1985). Retrieved on May 17, 2018 from https://songselect.ccli.com/Songs/177925/i-am-yours-you-are-mine.

 Morgan James makes all of our titles available
through the Library for All Charity Organization.

www.LibraryForAll.org